Please renew/return this item by the last date shown.

So that your telephone call is charged at local rate,
please call the numbers as set out below:

	From Area codes 01923 or 0208:	From the rest of Herts:
Renewals:	01923 471373	01438 737373
Enquiries:	01923 471333	01438 737333
Minicom:	01923 471599	01438 737599

L32b

11/12

L33

KITTY GODFREE

Lady of a Golden Age

HELEN WILLS DRAWS MRS. GODFREE—A STAR SHE BEAT.

THE FINISH OF A BACKHAND DRIVE: MRS. GODFREE, THE ENGLISH HOPE, IN PLAY—BY HELEN WILLS.

KITTY GODFREE

Lady of a Golden Age

GEOFFREY GREEN

THE KINGSWOOD PRESS

The Kingswood Press
an imprint of William Heinemann Ltd.
10 Upper Grosvenor Street, London W1X 9PA

LONDON   MELBOURNE
JOHANNESBURG   AUCKLAND

First published 1987

Typeset by Inforum Ltd, Portsmouth
Printed in Great Britain by Redwood Burn Ltd

Contents

Acknowledgements

The author and publisher would particularly like to thank Kitty God-free, David Godfree, Basil Hutchins and Alan Little of The Wimbledon Lawn Tennis Museum, Dan Maskell and Nicholas Keith, for their support and enthusiasm.

Foreword By Dan Maskell

It was one morning in the summer of 1924 that I was required to attend Mr Nolly Noel, the famous Secretary of Queen's Club, in his office. Having joined the club as a junior ballboy and then begun developing to be a teaching tennis professional, I wondered what I had done wrong to be called up, as I thought, on the mat.

To my relief and surprise, instead of a dressing-down, Mr Noel offered me two tickets for the Ladies Final at Wimbledon that afternoon. 'Take one of your colleagues with you,' he said. I had actually visited Wimbledon earlier, but never to see a match. When I told my father of the great, new centre court built there, he had remarked: 'Twelve thousand people round a tennis court! They must be mad. It will become a white elephant . . .'

A young colleague named Ernest Hunn accompanied me there and I still remember the number of the seat I had – D11 – near the entrance to the centre court. That was the first time I saw Mrs Godfree, or Miss McKane as she was then, before her marriage. She won a stirring match that afternoon against Miss Helen Wills, the American champion, but, in spite of the exciting ebb and flow of the game, what struck me particularly as a teaching professional was the way Miss McKane used her thumb along the back of her racket for back-hand strokes. Later on, I noted that the great French champion, Jean Borotra, employed the same grip for his backhand. That is what lingered in my memory for years. Most other first class players placed the thumb across or around the handle.

By 1929, I had become senior professional to the L.T.A. and the All-England Club at Wimbledon. One day in 1930, Mrs Godfree, then married, approached me for a knock-up on one of Wimbledon's outer hard courts. Following a warm-up, she said: 'I'd like to practice my lob'. That was the first time anyone had asked me to practise that stroke.

At the end Mrs Godfree said: 'Do you mind, Mr Maskell, if I suggest something to improve your smash? Use your wrist more freely to bring the racket head through with a swish, disturbing the air. You'll find it easier to practise with a lighter badminton racket.' She demonstrated how I tended to push the racket head at the ball, which did not make a swishing noise, and how 'throwing' it with a loose wrist did.

That's precisely what I did, taking the strings out. So involved did I become in this stroke that I used to take the badminton racket up to my bedroom, practising the stroke night and morning in my pyjamas. Since then, I have coached many beginners – even Davis Cup players – in this swish of the racket head for a smash, and, of course, for the service too. Years later Mrs Godfree, by then twice a Wimbledon champion, said to me: 'I must apologise for being so rude to you as a professional at Wimbledon all that time ago'. By then our friendship had already been cemented.

About ten years ago, I took a movie film of her in action playing in the members' Doubles tournament at Wimbledon and noted how she moved her feet and body instinctively to line up the ball at her side for a stroke, and not just reaching out her racket for short balls, especially short second services. These are the clues of good tennis.

I believe Mrs Godfree was one of the first British players to develop an all-court game, completing a deep ground stroke approach shot with a finishing volley, a tactic years later developed and improved by Alice Marble and Martina Navratilova. But, beyond this, I suggest that her championship victories of 1924 and 1926 sowed the seeds of Wimbledon wins by Dorothy Round in the mid-1930s and, after the war, by Angela Mortimer, Ann Jones and Virginia Wade. The meeting in 1961 between Angela Mortimer and Christine Truman was the first all-British final for forty-seven years. She might even have influenced Fred Perry to his three consecutive Wimbledon triumphs in 1934, 1935 and 1936, his successes in the American championships and the winning of the Davis Cup for four years running in the 1930s. Mrs Godfree indeed, I feel, showed Britain the way in world tennis.

But, more than that, I believe that her good behaviour and sportsmanship have rubbed off on the modern woman player which in this competitive world is a fine advertisement for tennis. Of the 128 ladies in the championship, there is scarcely a word of complaint; of the 128 men, only a handful offend.

Yet, most remarkable is the fact that, at the age of ninety, Mrs Godfree still hits a ball on the tennis court, now and then with her old friend, the eighty-eight year old Borotra, to put younger players to shame. She has played the game in every sense, and at every age.

Dan Maskell
July 1986

Introduction

In June 1986 Wimbledon celebrated its centenary of championship play. It was at that point that the Duke of Kent, president of the All England Club, supported by his Duchess, suggested to 'Buzzer' Hadingham, the chairman, that this special occasion might be marked by inviting the oldest surviving singles champions, Mrs Kitty Godfree and Monsieur Jean Borotra, of 1924 and 1926, to present the trophies on the centre court to the ladies' and gentlemen's champions and runners-up.

So it was that Kitty handed over the gold-plated salver to Miss Martina Navratilova on July 5, 1986. In so doing she was touching the famous trophy for the first time on the centre court. On the following day, Borotra, one of France's incomparable 'four mustketeers' of the 1920s and 30s, presented the precious gold cup to Boris Becker, the precocious eighteen year old West German who had demolished Ivan Lendl, the world's No 1, to retain his title.

The two ceremonies provided a touching scene, especially as on both days the Duchess of Kent walked off the court arm in arm, first with Kitty Godfree and then with Borotra. Those of the modern generation, ignorant of the past, saw on television two sporting heroes of sixty years ago.

Kitty Godfree was certainly one of the oustanding all-round games players of the world in her time. She was singles champion of Wimbledon twice and beaten finalist in 1923; All-England badminton champion in 1920, 1921, 1922 and 1924; selected to play for England at lacrosse against Scotland in 1914, a match that was cancelled because of the outbreak of war; cricketer, golfer and winner of a medal from the

Ice Skating Association at the age of ten: her talents were manifold and
manifest. As the tennis press wrote of her in 1919: 'She is the find of the
year' and 'head and shoulders above the young players'.

The Chinese have a saying – every day is a new day. Saturday
January 11, 1986 certainly proved so for me. It was at a dinner party in
Chelsea, hosted by Louise Moller, that David Godfree suddenly said to
me: 'Would you write the life story of my mother, Kitty?' Instinctively,
without a moment's thought, I answered in the affirmative and in
those few seconds a door was opened on a new project.

Although I had known her late husband, Leslie Godfree, a Davis
Cup player of the past, I had never met Kitty. But broadly, I knew of
her feats and that, ninety years young, she had lived through the
dramatic changes of the twentieth century with a cheerful smile. The
longest lived ladies' Wimbledon champion was still playing doubles
there in the covered courts once or twice a month; she drove a faithful
Mini and shopped daily on her bicycle, a forty year old BSA which
Leslie had bought for her as a coming home present after the second
world war. All this, and her sporting achievements, told me that there
was a romantic story to be told.

Slowly the past and present unfolded. Dan Maskell, the BBC television voice of Wimbledon, agreed to write a foreword. He had known
Kitty for many years. Similarly Ted Tinling, the guru of ladies' tennis
fashion, gave me an insight into her character, and I learned that
Philippe Chartrier, of the International Tennis Federation and President of the French Lawn Tennis Federation, had invited her to Paris as
a guest of the French championships. This underlined the respect and
affection others held for her.

Research was gathered on a tape recorder; this revealed her extraordinary instant recall. Events that eluded her were checked in a
special volume of all her results from 1919 to 1935, a labour of love
prepared by Alan Little in the Wimbledon museum, and presented to
her by 'Buzzer' Hadingham, Chairman of the All England Tennis and
Croquet Club which was founded in 1868. To all this was added family
details provided by David Godfree, Kitty's elder son.

In one sense Kitty has emerged as something of a chameleon.
Christened Kathleen, she became Biddy to close friends and Kitty to a
wider public. But there are no such vagaries in her personality.
Friendly, ready with a laugh, she is English to the core with a sense of
fair play and retains an unassuming normality – she does not act like a
star.

A special breed and a vital person, she is the apex of a loving family unit of two sons and three grandchildren. Happiness and the ability to ride misfortunes must be one of the secrets of her longevity. Another would be the early support of a devoted father and mother who believed in fresh air and games based on the Latin proverb *mens sana in corpore sano*.

An article appeared in *The Bystander* of 1923 which throws some light on the young 'Biddy' (or 'Kitty') McKane. It was headed 'Popular Personalities' and written by a *nom de plume* 'Paul Pry'. Ignoring the rather staid style of those days there is no missing the fact that Kitty had won many hearts through her sportsmanship and avoidance of publicity.

To be pre-eminently the finest all-round woman athlete in the British Isles is something of an achievement. I doubt if there is a woman in any part of the world at the present time who is so remarkably good at so many games as 'Biddy' McKane. She has, of course, won a great popularity with the uninitiated British public by reason chiefly of her wonderful tennis. Some of us know her as a past mistress at other forms of sport also.

For instance, she is the greatest badminton singles player living. She is in quite a class by herself at this scientific and extremely fast game. Having won the All-England championship for four years running – at which she met all the best women players there are, at the Logan Club (the MCC of the game) – she gives the Cup back again, and does not retain it proudly as most people would.

She is an international lacrosse player; an exhibition figure skater, championship class; a first-rank hockey player, and a golfer. There is no doubt that if she had time she would be equally good at any other ball game she took up.

Add to this the fact that she is entirely without a vestige of 'side' about any of the games she plays; that she loathes being photographed, and that she refuses utterly to be interviewed; and you have a very remarkable and unusual personality.

I personally am not so interested in the fact that she learned her tennis at St Andrews, as a schoolgirl; nor that she learned her badminton during the Christmas holidays in the club beneath the flat where I live; nor that it was at the Kew Tennis Club where she first began to shine as a young player, a very short time ago. What interests me more than all these things is the attitude she maintains about the whole business of fame. She tries to creep away from it.

If a deathly hush fell upon the centre court at Wimbledon when I strolled into it; or if I was besieged all the time by the ubiquitous authograph hunter, I should require an outsize in the largest hat sold. Not so Biddy. And human nature being what it is, that is, to my mind, a very peculiar thing. And yet not peculiar if you know the woman. With her it is *the game that matters*. There is no other consideration within her reckoning. Time and again I have seen her lose a match of doubles at tennis and badminton, and every time she has made it clear to her partner that it was *her* fault, when usually the contrary has been the case. She has never been known to mind losing, however great the issue.

You cannot find anyone who can tell you truthfully that they have ever seen her 'rattled'. For Biddy to lose her temper at a game is a thing unknown.

Her outstanding attraction is her complete simplicity where a game is concerned, at which she excels above most other people. There are no 'frills'. She genuinely enjoys every game in every place she plays: at any time, with any person however mediocre they may be as compared with her. What she suddenly feels like when confronted with Suzanne Lenglen, and the whole English tennis world mouthing silent prayers round the court, who can say? She certainly shows no outward and visible sign of the torment that must rage within. But it is quite certain that when this time comes again she will put up the best show for us that is possible to be given in England at the moment, in the most thoroughly sporting manner.

Biddy is, in fact, 'a sportsman' universally acknowledged. Few of us desire a higher title. None of us deserve it more.

Now though much older and wiser she remains intrinsically the same. Life, we learn, is the little shadow that sneaks across the lawn and melts into the sunset. Perhaps Kitty caught that little shadow in the grass and kept it from the going down of the sun. Maybe that's the secret of it all.

To look at her long life is to capture something of the past; she is a marvellous representative of an age departed.

1

Childhood

Kitty Godfree was born on May 7, 1896, at St Petersburgh Place, near the Kensington Gardens entrance to the Broadwalk. Her first memory is of being pushed in a pram, with her sister Margaret, by the nanny into the park. There they would meet other nannies and children and watch the toy boats being sailed on the Round Pond. Kitty also recalls a liking for Peter Pan; this apparently lasted until the family moved to Henley-on-Thames at the turn of the century, when she was four years of age. These fragments of a long past childhood come from the last days of Queen Victoria's long reign, but they are still clear in Kitty's mind.

The sisters' mother and father were a devoted couple which helped to make the girls' childhood a happy time. There was an age difference of some twenty years between the parents: she was young, delightfully gay, friendly, keen on bridge and badminton. And it was to their mother that the sisters were more closely drawn, probably because their father was a hard worker and they simply saw less of him. He, born John McKane, wore a beard, which was slightly frightening; and in true Victorian style he was something of a disciplinarian, albeit a benign one. He was a businessman who had built up a firm which manufactured pianos in Berlin and then imported them from Berlin for the English market, and exported them to various parts of the world.

Kitty's father, born in 1848, was the oldest of four children, three boys and a girl. Unfortunately his father, Kitty's grandfather, whom she never met, behaved badly towards his family so that at the age of fifteen, John McKane left his home in Hawick on the borders. He set out, with the proverbial shilling in his pocket and headed for London to 'seek fame and fortune'.

He found lodgings and a job. The latter was as a junior in the accounts department of a London store in Oxford Street. He acquired this position because he was good at figures. He continued in this job, gradually earning promotions and pay rises, and, all the while, making friends and getting to feel comfortable in the capital city.

Then one day, as he was leaving his office for lunch, he became aware of a fierce argument between two gentlemen on the pavement, very close to the road where the horse drawn buses were plying their trade. He stopped to listen and soon got the gist of this argument; one man was accusing the other of not paying for two pianos which he had bought.

After a short while John McKane stepped forward to the two gentleman, apologised for interrupting, said he couldn't help over-hearing and asked the appropriate gentleman how much he wanted for the pianos and whether he would allow him to buy them. This action caused a certain surprise, but the gentleman selling the pianos showed a great interest in the young stranger and, taking an instant liking to him, told him what he wanted for the pianos – twenty guineas each.

The deal was agreed and John McKane bought his first two pianos. At that time John had a friend with whom he played tennis and who had a house with a large basement. It was agreed that the pianos could be stored in the basement until such time as they could be sold.

Because of this chance meeting in Oxford Street in 1864, and the purchase of the pianos, which incidentally were sold for a handsome profit, John McKane decided that pianos would be his business. He continued working at his job while saving hard for his venture. Then, in 1869, having made previous contact with the manufacturers of these two pianos whose name he learned when they were in his possession, he packed his bag and set out for the first time to Berlin to meet Herr Alfred Ghast and Son.

Both father and son were brilliant craftsmen and tuners, but had little business acumen. John McKane persuaded them that he would be responsible for selling their pianos and would start off by buying their product as an agent and selling them from London. An agree-ment was reached and he started selling successfully. In time he started putting money into the company and he changed its name to 'Waldemar', a company of which he was the senior partner.

He had friends in Australia and Tasmania and, having contacted them by letter to first explain his ideas, he followed this up by travelling to those countries in 1873-4. He took two or three 'Waldemar' pianos with him. As a result of his efforts the business grew and grew. He, like all businessmen, had ups and downs. On one occasion he lost some uninsured pianos in a shipwreck (the ship sailed on a Friday!) but generally things went well.

And it was during this steadily prosperous phase of his life, in 1892 precisely, that John McKane married May Rawson, Kitty's mother. May was born on May 11th, 1873, the eldest of nine children; there were originally ten, but one died aged three, so when Kitty was born she was christened Kathleen after her mother's little sister. May's parents were tea planters in Assam, who had a London house in Chiswick. Being the eldest of such a large family, May was often left to look after all her brothers and sisters. She eventually got fed up with this and so left home at the age of fifteen to get a job as a children's nanny and teacher. She was fulfilling a very similar role to the one she had left at home, but being paid made all the difference!

She stayed with her first appointment for several years. It was in 1892 that she went with the family for their summer holiday to the Petersham Hotel, overlooking the river Thames, just outside Richmond and its famous Royal Park.

The hotel had a tennis court and staying at the hotel were two gentlemen who used to play regularly. One of these was John McKane, the other, the friend who had allowed him to store his first two pianos in his basement.

John McKane noticed May Rawson, who was a very pretty young girl, and ensured that they got to know one another.

Romance blossomed and they were married around Christmas 1892, when May was nearly twenty and John McKane was forty-four years of age. Margaret was born in April 1895 and Kitty a year after that.

So the girls who were to become champions in several sports were born as a result of a romance at the old Petersham Hotel, a hotel that sadly no longer stands.

As the girls grew up a governess was employed to see to their welfare and education. Meanwhile the piano business progressed greatly, both in Great Britain and in the Empire.

The McKanes were a happy family. They lived in Henley for five years, years during which father showed great pride in his two girls. He lost no opportunity in doing what he could for them. He had two small bicycles built and the children used to hare round the lawn and flower beds of their large garden. Henley and Marlow Regattas used to be visited every summer; the parents loved living near the Thames, a feeling that rubbed off on the two girls. Henley proved the happiest home of those early years.

The Henley days were also enhanced by a governess, a Miss Willett. She was a young woman in her twenties, virtually the same age as May, Kitty's mother.

Margaret and Kitty both loved the gentle, kind and clever Miss Willett who, Kitty now says, probably got the most out of her young charges because they were ever eager to please her. But the day of parting duly came. John McKane announced that his daughters would shortly be going to school in London and Miss Willett, looking ahead, said that she already had been offered a position to teach two daughters of an MP, Josia Wedgwood. That was the friendly ending to a happy relationship.

So off the family went to London. Margaret, the elder by a year, and Kitty, went to the Froebel Institute at Barons Court. After a year there came one at St Pauls School. It was around this time that Miss Willett came to see John McKane to ask his advice on a problem. Although the father was an agnostic, and Miss Willett religious, they respected each other's opinions. The governess explained that she and Wedgwood, her new employer, had fallen in love and he wanted to marry her. But because Wedgwood was still with his wife McKane said that a divorce would be out of the question. McKane suggested that she go as far away as possible. Because he knew of a family in Hobart, Tasmania, he said he would try to arrange a position for her there.

So bravely Miss Willett departed to the Southern Cross. But the story did not end there. After twenty years she received a telegram from Josia Wedgwood saying that his wife had died and would she return. This she did. They were married and had twenty years of happiness. By then she was stone deaf but Kitty and Margaret kept in touch with her until she died aged ninety. From five years old until she was eighty Kitty kept the fires of friendship and affection burning.

Margaret and Kitty were healthy children. Daily cold baths from the earliest years probably accounted for this. Margaret, nicknamed Peggie, lived to be eighty-nine, while Kitty is now into her nineties; perhaps this is a good advertisement for cold baths and a loving, close-knit family life. Although Kitty gained most of the major sporting honours in the family, Margaret was no slouch. She once won the All-England badminton singles title, and also won the doubles with her sister. She reached a Wimbledon doubles final with Kitty, in 1922, and was an outstanding golfer. Added to which both Margaret and Kitty married sportsmen in later life – Margaret to Andrew Denys Stocks, a hockey international, and Kitty to Leslie Godfree, a Davis Cup tennis player.

A particular sporting treat of childhood was to go to Switzerland just after Christmas. For consecutive years, Kitty from the age of five, they made tracks to a small place named Grindelwald. Here was a wide valley from which the sun did not disappear behind the mountain until after four o'clock. It was in this valley that they took up skiing, tobogganing, and ice skating. On the sixth year, by which time Kitty was twelve and Margaret thirteen, Mrs McKane met a young lady with whom she became friendly. This new friend was Beryl Hawtry, a niece of Charles Hawtry, the actor. She had recently left St Leonards School, at St Andrews in Scotland, and she suggested that the bracing climate there might be very suitable for Margaret. At that stage Margaret was suspected of having glandular fever and her specialist had prescribed such an outdoors climate. Two or three letters to the authorities and it was agreed that both girls should go to St Leonards.

The school was a girls' public school run very much on the lines of similar boys' institutions such as Eton and Winchester. There were eight houses, prefects, heads of houses, and fagging, but no beating. Lines or being sent to bed early were the main punishments. Margaret went straight into the senior school where there were some 250 girls, but Kitty, just twelve, had to spend a year in the junior school before joining her sister.

All had been arranged from Switzerland. From St Moritz, to London, and then to St Andrews and St Leonards School, arriving in scarlet kilts and white tops while waiting for their proper school uniforms to arrive from London. No entrance exam had to be passed; the sisters, with their skating, skiing and the rest obviously had sport in their blood, and were accepted by a school which had a strong accent on physical education and games.

Perhaps their applications to join the sport-minded school included reference to events of some three years earlier, around 1905–6. This was an epic bicycle ride from London to Berlin. John McKane, announcing that he needed to meet his partner in Germany, suggested that the whole family might bicycle there. The girls could ride well, were strong enough and seemed capable of facing the 600 mile journey. Miss Willett was also agreeable to the idea and so one day the cavalcade, having sent luggage ahead, set out from their flat opposite Barkers store in Kensington High Street.

What a charming picture they must have made, mounted and dressed in Edwardian attire: a bearded father and four females – an attractive young wife, a young governess, and two young daughters. Attaching various pieces of clothing to their bikes for the journey they headed for Harwich and crossed by boat to the Hook of Holland. The whole operation was planned with military precision. Thirty miles a day was the aim, allowing for weather, punctures and other possible repairs.

They stayed at inns every night and rode through Holland and Belgium on the way, acres of tulips providing a lasting memory for Biddy. A weekend was spent with a distant aunt in Cologne and they had some days sightseeing in the beautiful Hartz mountains.

After three weeks, Berlin was reached. The whole journey had seen no major mishap. In those days motor cars were few and far between and traffic was mostly horse drawn. The children stood the journey well but were happy for some relaxation at the premises the father had arranged in advance.

Scheduled to stay in Berlin for eight weeks Margaret and Kitty, with Miss Willett, made the zoo their target. There was a lot to see there and many games to play. They were pleased with the situation. But after six weeks Mrs McKane became bored. She missed her friends in London and her badminton and, with Mr McKane's agreement, the four girls made for home. They returned by train, leaving John behind for a fortnight to complete his piano business. He, too, returned by train.

The end of the Waldemar Piano Co. came on August 14, 1914, the day the first world war broke out. John McKane was never to see or hear of the Ghast family again. John himself was sixty-eight years of age in 1914 and the shock of events affected his health. After the war, when reparations were being made, he never actually put in his bid because, by 1920, he was seventy-four and felt just too old and tired to apply.

The factory in Germany had been used as a munitions factory and all the wood working equipment had been removed and presumably destroyed. However, one thing that John McKane still had in his possession were the designs for the front panels of these Waldemar pianos. When he learned that the factory was no more, he decided to adapt those attractive designs and have them modified and made up into fabric. In fact it was May McKane's brother, Charles Rawson, who had been a very clever engineer and lived at Marlow, who designed the conversion from the pattern on the piano panel to the material for soft furnishings. These were so successful that when John McKane approached Harvey Nichols with his design, they were readily accepted. This small return was to renew his interest in business life after 1920.

2

S c h o o l d a y s

It was 1909 when Margaret, aged fourteen, and Kitty, not yet quite thirteen, started their schooling in Scotland. And although they didn't know it as they joined the Flying Scotsman at King's Cross some very exciting and memorable events lay ahead of them. Being a boarder was quite new to them but it was an experience they were to enjoy at St Leonards School.

Apart from normal academic lessons, there was a wide range of activities at the school – music, art, acting and orchestral outlets. But the important accent was on outdoor activities, largely sport. It was an attitude of the school on which the sisters McKane thrived.

In addition to the games Kitty particularly enjoyed art and she was also involved in playing the piano and the mandolin. It was in both these extra pursuits – on which considerable time and money was spent – that Kitty had two memorable experiences.

It was after a couple of years in the senior school that it was decided that Kitty was capable of playing a piano solo at a school concert. She was not happy at the decision and was convinced she would break down when the time came. For a fortnight there was little else on her mind. It caused considerable anxiety to herself as she repeatedly told her piano teacher that she was not up to it. She pleaded to be excused. 'Don't be silly, girl, of course you can do it' was the only answer she received as she continued to work herself into a state.

Then a small miracle occurred. The very day before the concert a young girl in one of the other houses was struck down by scarlet fever and the whole school was evacuated and temporarily closed. Margaret and Kitty went home, Kitty counting every lucky star on the way. To this day she breathes a sigh of relief at the memory of that escape.

At another concert Kitty was called up to play her mandolin in a quartet involving two violins and a viola. Having practised solemnly beforehand she felt as ready as she could expect when the big night at last arrived. Nerves were stretched like guitar strings as the head girl was attending to the stage curtain. Then it happened. Kitty dropped the plectrum for her mandolin. She searched for it frantically below her chair. But in the back stage gloom she was defeated. In a panic she mumbled to the head girl who was about to draw back the curtains: 'I've lost my plectrum'. 'Oh, you silly girl,' came the reply, 'here, use my hairpin'. An example of quick thinking and the situation was saved. No-one guessed that a hairpin was a substitute for a plectrum as 'The Bluebells of Scotland' echoed musically through a hall full of applause.

Kitty was next roped in to take part in a couple of plays. The first was *Quality Street* in which her role was that of a house maid. Removing a tea tray from the drawing room set she had to close the door behind her with her foot. The script had the mistress saying angrily: 'Mabel, how many times must I tell you not to slam the door with your foot. Close it gently with your hand.' The school, not realising it was all part of the play and thinking Kitty was being ticked off, roared with laughter and applauded her when next she appeared.

Then followed the part of a soldier in a battle scene in *Cyrano de Bergerac*. One of the older girls was chosen as Cyrano and, having a *retroussé* nose, had her proboscis suitability built up for the traditional role. A couple of men who looked after the grounds were also dragooned into the play to take part in the battle scene.

One of the mistresses, who obviously had some experience as a producer, organised this scene very realistically. When the dramatic moment came, so loud were the screams of 'dying' and so loud the firearms of the two groundsmen that the hall was almost completely filled with noise and smoke. It all seemed so real that the audience, which included parents from St Andrews, all but fled. Kitty thoroughly enjoyed that evening.

Art was one of her favourite subjects, especially when it led to excursions to etch old buildings in St Andrews during the summer term. But with art, as with other things, Kitty tended to be forgetful. With a five or six minute walk between her house and the classroom too often she left a required book behind and would have to hurry to retrieve it. Each such occasion would cost a black mark which could rebound on her dormitory. Three black marks a week in all and the dormitory would miss a week's issue of sweets. One can imagine the feelings of the rest of the girls when this happened. But perhaps because Kitty was so good at games they would control their grumbles. 'In this ability to forget I was an enemy to myself' she recalls.

Still Kitty did enough work to take the Oxford and Cambridge Higher Certificate exam when she was almost eighteen. She passed in three subjects – maths, algebra and geometry, but failed in trigonometry. Three passes out of four was fair but not good enough and she failed to procure her Higher Certificate. But at least it showed she had done *some* work.

Two other schoolday memories still linger on. On one occasion she visited the school house for a party. While enjoying the company she was shown a corner of the hall. 'That's where a wicked nun was walled up years ago and her ghost still appears on Hallowe'en Night', she was told – a grizzly kind of story enjoyed by the young. Fact or fiction it left its mark on Kitty for many years.

One Easter weekend she was invited by a girl in her house to stay in a fisherman's cottage taken by her parents in a lovely area on the north-east coast of Scotland. There were one or two other guests there, too, one of whom was the girl's brother. He was twenty years of age and owned a new steam motor car. Setting out one day to attend a highland sports meeting Kitty and the brother were tootling along a narrow country road when they came round a bend to see two horses drawing a cart and driver coming towards them. Not very exciting one might think, but there was no room to pass and the approaching horses were fast asleep! Sleep-walking horses may be bizarre but perhaps not so odd as the fact that the driver was also fast asleep – all of them affected by a hot summer's day.

There was no escape. On came the sleeping trio quite oblivious of what was about to happen. And happen it did – a head-on collision. It all happened at a modest speed but fast enough for the steam boiler of the brother's car to be damaged. The cart driver, of course, woke up with a torrent of coarse language which did nothing to help the burst boiler of the brother's car. However, being something of an engineer he managed to patch up affairs; but two hours of a lovely summer's afternoon were lost and they never did get to the highland meeting.

'It really was a very good school' recalls Kitty. 'There was so much to do there and anyone who showed interest in things was thoroughly encouraged. The staff were always interested in the person.' There were two women, both trained at a Swedish college, who took gym. There were also two good, young games mistresses who looked after most of the sports. Cricket was considered the senior game, followed by hockey, lacrosse, tennis, golf and Eton fives.

The playing fields were very extensive, a large plateau which could cater for four cricket matches at the same time; there were also four hockey pitches which were used in the winter term and turned to lacrosse after Christmas. Eton fives was the least important sport while tennis came only second to cricket in the summer. Despite this there were four hard courts and four grass, although only one of the latter was considered playable.

Since there were few schools close by available for competition most of the games were based on house matches. Eton fives, played with both hands, was very unpopular, particularly with the piano teachers. Several pupils would suffer from damaged hands which would cause great annoyance: 'You can't practise today because you've been playing that stupid game,' was the cry.

There was a silver cup for each sport to be won by a house and proudly displayed on a mantelpiece. Unfortunately for the rest of the school Kitty's house won every cup for every one of the five years she was there, except the hockey trophy lost for the first time in her last year. 'We played all games seriously but had great fun doing so. But don't imagine that I was responsible for all this success. Far from it. It's just that we had a talented house and a house mistress who was herself keen on games and encouraged everyone.'

'Typical of this was why we lost the hockey trophy – to everyone else's delight and my sadness.' Kitty's house team had reached the final again but on that occasion the house mistress was absent from the school, recovering from an appendix operation. 'It's not that we slacked off in her absence. Far from it. Just the opposite in fact. We were so anxious to win for her that it affected our play. It was psychological.'

The house, the favourites, lost 1–0. The winners played very well, preparing their tactics carefully and marking Kitty at centre forward so closely that she didn't get a shot in the whole match.

It was around this time that some twins – Billie and Elza Garvey – who were to become life-long friends, arrived in the house from India.

Aged sixteen, they arrived rather later than usual because they had come from India where their father was in the army. Both were good at cricket and both were very musical. Margaret and Kitty soon hit it off with them.

The cricket shield had almost found a permanent home in their house as it was won for the fifth year in succession. In her last year Margaret made two centuries. She had style and was never in a hurry; by way of contrast, Kitty was always charging about in a mood of hit or miss. But Kitty, too, ran up a century in her last summer, hitting 136 not out. Coaching that their father had organised for them at Hambledon years earlier paid dividends.

But coaching at cricket was not all the father arranged. Learning that golf was another game played at St Leonards – and at St Andrews of all places, the Rome of golf – he arranged for them to be coached at the world famous club. They were sent to the professional's shop where Willie Auchterlonie, winner of the ancient open golf tournament, took them in hand.

They did not play on the holy of holies, of course. Indeed they were not even allowed into the hallowed perimeters but the location must have helped. Margaret, who had helped Kitty to win the house tennis just before she left school, trained to be a useful golfer with a handicap of five with the Ladies Golf Union.

With Margaret departed there was a hole left in the house where golf was concerned. However, there was a good player left – Jean, a girl with a weak heart and thus not allowed to play running games. The problem was to find a partner for Jean. They decided to try out Kitty, knowing that she had received coaching from Willie Auchterlonie.

A couple of trial runs round the edge of St Andrews and Jean, a good player, passed final judgement: 'She can't be worse than any of the others.' So, off they started. A long walk through the town of St Andrews was the prelude to a first round victory. When they repeated the success in round two, surprise and interest began to grow. Win number three saw them into the final and the excitement grew joyously.

For the climax they were sent off to the first tee in a horse and carriage. This was royal treatment. Jean played beautifully – as she had done in every round. Kitty putted tightly, sufficiently well for her partner to sink the vital shots. As a result they were home – the champions. A ride back in the horse and carriage and a noisy reception at the front door led to a special tea party in the house mistress's private room. To this the head girl was also invited; it was a friendly, enjoyable finish to a surprising victory.

But as Kitty now says: 'Trying to hit and control a stationary ball used to make me angry. I always preferred a moving ball game.' She was right handed for hockey, tennis and golf, left handed at cricket and lacrosse and writing, and played both handed at fives. Later, when she had left school, Kitty was right handed at badminton.

Circumstances denied both Kitty and Margaret international caps at lacrosse. It was in the 1914 season that they were selected by Scotland to play England, (because they were at a Scottish school). Having made their choice the selectors then changed their minds, thinking that, as schoolgirls, they would be too young to face the challenge, Kitty and Margaret were withdrawn from the team.

At this the English selectors pricked up their ears and were on the point of considering their ability when the first world war broke out. That was that; but they were virtual internationals.

This was the finale of five very happy and successful years at a fine school. It also marked the end of an important period of Kitty's life as she entered her eighteenth year. She had learned discipline, manners and respect for other human beings and, although she found it strange being separated from home at the start, she had settled in a new life and learned how to discover one's own level quickly – a lesson she never forgot.

3

The First World War — and Work

Two weeks after Kitty left St Leonards the first world war began. Turmoil reigned as young men, the flower of a generation, joined the armed forces. Many of them were to lose their lives in the murky and muddy trenches that were the battlefields of Europe. At the same time women searched for jobs to do in the emergency – to make their contribution to the war effort.

Again Margaret and Kitty were lucky. They met a woman employed in the War Office pensions department who said to their mother that if the girls wanted a job she could use them. It was a sad fact that there would be a growth of work now that the war had begun.

Thus, inside a week, the sisters found themselves on the staff of the pensions fund doing useful work. Disabled and semi-disabled soldiers, examined by doctors, relied on the War Office for pensions and, as the casualties grew, the work of the department mounted. At that time the department had their offices at Baker Street, but after a couple of years it was found necessary to look for larger premises.

Kitty's family then lived at 43 Berners Street, a house bought by her father and converted into four flats, two of which were let to businessmen. Mother and father lived on the first floor, and the sisters slept in the top flat which the father used occasionally as an office for his piano work. The loss of contact with Berlin, due to the war, was a grievous blow to the McKanes but Berners Street at least was convenient for the Baker Street job.

The larger premises for the pensions people proved to be the lake in St James's Park. It was drained and filled with nissen huts. And useful though the work was, two years of office and paper work was as much as Kitty's lively spirit could stand. She longed for the wide open spaces and some physical action. During this grey period she had joined the Kew Lawn Tennis Club and was lucky enough to meet there a Mr Black, manager of the Ford Motor Co. repair shop and depôt.

While Margaret – always the calmer and steadier in temperament, in contrast to Kitty's vitality and 'get up and go' – worked on to reach a responsible position in the pensions department, Kitty broke loose to join Ford and feel the fresh air. Her duties were now far more to her taste. She found herself having to drive 'tin lizzies' and vans which arrived in a steady flow at the Ford Depôt at Brook Green.

Kitty had no licence and now confesses she could not even drive. But being an adventurous character she let nothing stand in her way. A few lessons from a man at the depôt quickly got her started and with a first, top and reverse gear, brake, horn, and steering wheel she was off. 'Those tin lizzies were so easy to drive,' she now says with a laugh. She was once caught speeding in Roehampton Lane but managed to talk her way out of trouble.

The daily job was to drive the newly arrived cars from Brook Green to the Robin Hood Gate at Richmond Park. There was a steep hill, known as 'Test Hill' just inside the park. A convoy of six or seven men and four or five girls would drive to this rendezvous where a Mr Carpenter, the organiser, would meet two representatives from the War Office.

The vehicles that could not negotiate the hill would be turned down, but the others would be passed and bought for the War Office to be shipped to the forces in France, having first been driven on to Hurst Park race course which had become a departure depôt.

While Kitty was busy with her work her father's piano business was on its last legs. After so many years of hard work this was a tragedy but, being part Scottish and part Irish, he and his wife were not to be beaten. They moved to a flat off the Gloucester Road, next door to the Logan Badminton Club – the premier location and administrative base of the game.

The McKanes organised a residential bridge club where the young, lively mother proved an ideal hostess while the father looked after the administrative paperwork in a separate office in the flat. The difficult days of economies and privations had arrived but the club had to provide a living for the McKane family during the war years.

The war years were difficult for the McKane family but perhaps they counted themselves lucky in not having sons to send to the conflict. For the women in the family, as for women throughout Britain, 1914–1918 proved to be years of new experiences and new responsibilities. And Kitty was one who, at the same time as feeling grief and despair over the destruction of a generation, found the first world war to be a personal watershed in life.

4

C h a n g e

Touched by the final years of the Victorian age, Kitty had grown up in the Edwardian era which many would regard as the golden period of peace and comfort. It was also a time of hope and of new inventions. The wireless, aeroplane and motor car were all developed during this period.

Notably too, there was a breakthrough from Victorian conventions, achieved largely in the arts: the triumph of the Russian ballet and the raucous arrival of ragtime typified this. At the same time there was social controversy and ferment, strikes and suffragettes. Kitty's memory retains a flavour of these times.

Without being conscious of it, her adolescent life was surrounded and perhaps governed, by class consciousness. Although the glitter of rank and wealth was not confined to Britain – it was much the same story in Paris, Rome and Vienna – the British occupied and decorated the central stage and did most to create the idea of the golden age.

Many things combined to stoke the legend. Not least among them was that King Edward VII restored the home of the monarchy to London when he lit up Buckingham Palace and flung it open to rich financiers. They added their wealth to that of the great families of landowners. Income tax was the equivalent of 2p in the pound; direct taxation was still so low that it could be virtually ignored. The cost of living was small for the well-to-do and domestic servants, on whom society depended, could be hired for absurdly small wages.

However, Kitty was not of that grand world and she certainly would not have been interested in it. She belonged to the middle class, a world of successful manufacturers, merchants, solicitors, physicians, surgeons, property owners and speculators. It was also a world of set patterns of behaviour – regular church attendance, voting for the Tory party, living in large houses and expecting very different lives for men and women. The rules of the class structure were rigidly adhered to in these circles, and not least at one of the middle and upper classes' favourite institutions, the tennis party.

Kitty's early life in tennis has to be seen within the context of this class consciousness. Things, of course, have changed. Kitty herself has seen five monarchs and an abdication as well as countless technological and social developments; but to understand her early life we have to try to grasp exactly how strong the idea of class, with all its ramifications, really was. And where better to get our history lesson than on the tennis court?

Tennis before the first war, and up to the middle 1930s, possessed an ethos. It was a social game, a plaything for the upper and middle classes. Private tennis parties were the vogue. At first the wealthy owned grass or hard courts, but as the advancing years brought a greater expense in upkeep so many of the former began to decline before eventually being left fallow.

There was a snobbishnes about those tennis parties. Tea and cucumber sandwiches were very much a part of the scene. The general standard of play was mediocre but fun and enjoyment were the ruling aims. Considered as a poor relation of cricket, tennis was regarded as a game of 'pat and giggle'.

Yet, while cricket prospered in the confines of the Empire – in Australia, New Zealand, India, Ceylon, South Africa and eventually the West Indies – it was tennis that spread wider through the globe and took root more seriously in many countries of Europe. Like association football, tennis became one of Britain's widest exports.

In April 1919 tennis got on its feet again after the war, and it was then that Kitty began her competitive career, at Roehampton. For the first year it was uncomfortable going. She was the new girl in an experienced company of ladies, most of whom had travelled the country from tournament to tournament before 1914 and did not relish the youthful challenge to their seniority. Kitty hardly knew any of them, married women with well-off husbands.

Kitty's father by now had totally lost his piano business and was in hard straits, which sadly told on Kitty's role in this new found society. The matrons did not exactly ignore the new girl but they certainly did their best to keep her in her place. When she began to beat some of them a touch of jealousy crept in. Coming from a loving family where affection was the key note, she found this unfriendly attitude both distasteful and surprising. But, being a natural games player, she generally rose above it and finally fought through to a rightful place in the company. She put a few noses out of joint when she was selected to represent England in the world covered court championship in Paris within seven months of having joined the tennis 'jungle'. But by then she had won the doubles at the Gipsy Club in North London and had taken three singles titles at Frinton, Bournemouth in the Hampshire championships and at Hythe in the Kent Coast championships. In the process she had beaten three married women, Mrs Winch, Mrs Crad-dock and Mrs Satterthwaite, in the respective finals.

Acceptance by the matrons could not be denied when in the August of the next year, 1920, Kitty was selected for the Olympic Games in Antwerp. She proceeded to win a gold medal in the doubles, a silver in the mixed and a bronze for third place in the singles. By now she had truly won her spurs.

But still one stumbling block remained. This was Elizabeth Ryan, the American, four years her senior, who had settled in England from California in 1912, and who had become the accepted headmistress of the company. Kitty ran into her in only her second senior match at Beckenham in April 1919. She lost, of course, and was to fail in each of her first six meetings with Ryan.

At last, in September 1921, nearly two and a half years since that opening at Beckenham, Kitty finally achieved her first victory over Ryan. It was at Hendon and a fine, close match ended in her favour, 3–6, 7–5, 8–6. When both of them finally retired in the 1930s, they had met twenty-one times with Kitty just in the lead by eleven wins to ten.

The early part of Kitty's tennis career brought one slight worry. Her father had got to know a director of J Lyons & Co, the caterers, who had suggested that if his daughter would like a job to help the finances she could work in the company's offices. This was accepted and for a year Kitty travelled to Greenford earning £2.50 per week. But whenever she played in a tournament she could leave early to take part. It was a perfectly honest, working agreement, but Kitty sensed that the Lawn Tennis Association were investigating the situation to make sure that she was not breaking their strict rules of amateurism. She perfectly understood their concern but knew that she was being honest and not stepping out of line.

It was during these awkward beginnings that she was befriended by a kind old gentleman of the All England Club committee. This was Alfred Egerton Maynard-Taylor, who became something of an adopted 'Dutch Uncle' giving advice in any problems. His son, Aldersey, later became the Club solicitor, a member and a good tennis player too. Another helpful friend proved to be Leo Maxe. He was middle aged when Kitty got to know him; he was a former Oxford half blue at tennis and had a private court at his house in Kensington. He was Editor of *The National Review* and had many friends who used his court. He was very kind to the sisters Margaret and Kitty who played there a lot. Kitty in particular sharpened her game against some good men.

One afternoon, at one of Leo's tennis parties, the maid came out to the garden. In a pitch of high excitement she announced that the Prince of Wales had arrived and asked if he could watch the tennis. Helen Wills was among the playing party and it became obvious that she was the one the Prince wished to meet.

Kitty cannot remember the year of this event – either 1924 or 1927, on one of Wills' early visits to Wimbledon – but in view of the Prince's later involvement with Mrs Simpson it was clear that he already had a sympathetic eye for an attractive American girl. Tea in the garden with the charming Prince of Wales was a memory to treasure.

Leo Maxe later underlined his friendship with the McKane sisters by leaving each of them £500 in his will, a helpful bounty, gratefully accepted.

Most of the domestic tournaments around the country not only held a main event but, concurrently, ran a handicap for those knocked out early in the main event. If Kitty ever decided to enter the lesser tournament she found that within the first summer her handicap had changed from plus fifteen to minus thirty! This represented an improvement of three points per game, a remarkable advance.

Tournaments in those days were fun, especially when enjoyed with friends. And it was with friends that Kitty and Margaret would stay on their trips around the country. As always it was expenses that had to be watched. It was a case of private houses rather than hotels, and lifts in motor cars rather than trains. All this was a great saving, especially with vouchers for the winners of the main events standing at only two or three pounds. Still, as Kitty now reflects, it was all great fun.

Scarborough, it seems, was most enjoyable. Kitty always stayed with a doctor and his family. She also enjoyed trips to tournaments in the Isle of Wight, but Buxton in Derbyshire was a test if the weather was bad. One of the highest points in the country, rain often spoiled the tournament. Not permitted to wear spikes, Kitty found it best to play with a couple of stockings on each shoeless foot.

It was during the winter months, when there were no facilities for playing tennis, that Kitty took to badminton to keep her eye in and to stay reasonably fit. She took to the game like a duck to water. She and Margaret had played during school holidays from St Leonards, but now it was the big time. In 1920, 21, 22 and 24 Kitty won the All England singles title. In those years she was virtually unbeatable. She eventually gave up in 1924, a retirement which ironically allowed Margaret to become the champion. Singles, doubles (with Margaret) and mixed (with Devlin, the Irishman) were all the same to her. One can imagine there was a sigh of relief from other badminton players when Kitty went away on tennis tours.

Looking back on it all now she remembers the fun, the many friends she met and the many places she visited. It was a gift she received from the game and something that would never otherwise have come her way. She can thank St Leonards School up in Scotland for putting her feet on the road, and Kew Lawn Tennis Club for beginning to hone her game.

In 1984, the All-England Club presented Kitty with a volume of match scores dating from her start in 1919 until her retirement in 1935. In the volume was a letter from 'Buzzer' Hadingham:

My dear Biddy, I thought it would be rather nice for you to have a complete record of ALL your matches and thanks to the diligence and enthusiasm of Alan Little, here it is! As your very privileged partner on many happy friendly mixed games in recent years, I am so glad to have this opportunity to say thank you for all you have done for the game we all love.

The total result is that in 17 years of competition Kitty won 46 singles titles and 107 doubles and mixed titles. Not bad for a natural left-hander forced to play with her right!

That volume of scores presented to Kitty remains a guide to the tournaments she played in the UK. No one could play in all these but in the main it could be regarded as a 'circuit' with the opposition predominantly British. None of the great foreign stars entered – no Suzanne Lenglen, Helen Wills or Mrs Mallory for instance, who each had their own competitions at home.

As a rule these circuits covered the summer months from April to September – Spring to Autumn in fact. Here is the complete list of Kitty's opening season in 1919 and includes everything except the All England championship at Worple Road held in June: Roehampton, Chiswick, Queen's Club, Norwood, Frinton, Bournemouth, Eastbourne, Scarborough, Hythe. In October and November there followed the London covered court championships and the World covered court championships in Paris. On the whole this was the domestic programme she followed from 1919 until she began to cut down her engagements in 1935. And while one is pleased to hear Kitty describe it all as 'fun', there was, of course, the element of competition. If Elizabeth Ryan, who Kitty eventually conquered, was her major rival in the home tournaments it was the great Suzanne Lenglen who became Kitty's great adversary in tournaments with an international entry. In the ladies' arena the British had held sway until the arrival of the brilliant French woman. In 1919 it was Lenglen who took the All England crown from Mrs Lambert Chambers, the pre-war holder of the singles, and it was Lenglen who was to dominate the next half dozen years. Virtually no-one could touch her.

Kitty was the only Briton able to offer any resistance to Lenglen's superiority during the 1920s. And in spite of the overpowering presence of the French woman Kitty bravely took the women's singles in 1924 and 1926 after being silenced by Suzanne in the final of 1923 by 6–2, 6–2. In 1919 Kitty lost to Lenglen in a quarter final, 6–0, 6–1 and in 1922 by 6–1, 7–5 in the first round. Seeding did not come into existence until 1927 so that it was bad luck that Kitty was drawn to face the French steamroller so often in those early championships.

5

Worple Road and Wimbledon

It was in 1919, shortly after the end of 'the war to end all wars' that Kitty, a young woman of 23, inexperienced in the 'jungle' of tournament tennis, made her bow in the championships organised by the All England Club. This was at Worple Road, the predecessor of Wimbledon. In the five years that were to follow she was to become a champion and an outstanding, popular figure with the man and woman in the street. Involved in her exciting life and aware merely of her new surroundings, she was only dimly aware of the history of the stage she strode. What had happened in the years before the war was of no more than passing interest.

For instance she scarcely realised that only 200 spectators, each paying one shilling entrance fee, watched the first final of all in 1877. The past was dead – only the future beckoned. She cannot now remember whether or not she was conscious of many facts – that women's singles started in 1884 when only thirteen competitors entered; that it was the same year that men's doubles began and that the winner of one year merely waited until the next to be challenged in the Challenge Round.

Certainly she would not have known of the disparaging remarks made by the winner of the first final, nor of the fact that the final itself was postponed for a few days because of the more important Eton v. Harrow cricket match at Lords.

In fact it was an Old Harrovian, Spencer Gore, who won that opening final but having done so wrote: 'Its want of variety will prevent lawn tennis in its present form from taking rank among our great games.'

As if this were not enough, the next winner, P Hadlow, who beat Gore in the 1878 final was a tea planter in Ceylon (now Sri Lanka). He entered the championship for a laugh, won the title and disappeared at once back to his plantation. It was scarcely an encouraging start for tennis and the All-England Croquet Club.

Early in its life, too, the club was in some financial difficulties which moved one of the famous Renshaw brothers, so often between them champions from 1881 to 1889, to help the club with a gift of £600.

Kitty played tournaments at Worple Road for only three years before the move was made to the much larger complex at Church Road, Wimbledon. Not being a member of the All-England Club in those days her memories are misty and fragmentary. But she recalls no great sadness or sentimentality at the change of championship venue.

To reach Worple Road one took a District line train to Wimbledon station and walked for fifteen minutes to the ground carrying one's bag of tennis clothes. Alternatively there was a slow suburban train from Waterloo which stopped at a wayside halt hear the ground. The fact expresses used to rattle through close to the courts; this was a nuisance to the players. Often, at the end of a rally, action would stop with enquiries of the umpire of the score or of the calls of linesman. The noise then, comparatively, must have been like the noise these days of aircraft at Flushing Meadow, New York, taking off from nearby Kennedy Airport.

There was a centre court with covered seating on three sides for 3500 spectators as well as nine other courts, four of them parallel to and fairly close to the disturbing railway line.

The men's dressing rooms were in the pavilion but the women faced something of a rough passage. The club bought two houses, adjacent to the ground, at a cost of £2,300 and converted them into ladies' dressing rooms and club offices. The women would emerge from the back door, walk through the back garden and enter the ground by way of the back gate. One cannot see the ladies of today putting up with such a procedure. •

To show how the popularity of the event had increased one can look at what happened at Worple Road in 1913. In perfect weather some 10,000 people suffocated the grounds. The unoffical asking price for watching the Challenge Round was about £7.50! 1913 was the year when two other events came about. First, the newly created International Lawn Tennis Federation granted the event the lofty title of the

'World Championship on Grass' – a title which was dispensed with by the Club in 1923 at the new Wimbledon. Second it was the year of bag searches at the gate! Earlier in that same year, on a rising tide of support, suffragettes had raided the ground with the result that visitors to Worple Road had their carrier bags and parcels scrutinised by the doormen. The shadows of coming events were cast over that summer before the war.

Because tennis then was very much a part of the upper and middle classes, so Worple Road was a Victorian and Edwardian fashion show, even amongst those who had to stand rather than sit. The tea lawn provided a sea of top hats; the ladies were very elegantly dressed with bustles and with large-brimmed flower hats.

As if to underline this class significance the Crown Princess Stephanie of Austria, the first Royal visitor to the championships, attended in 1895. In 1906 there came the Grand Duchess Anastasia and Grand Duke Michael of Russia to be followed, the very next year, by the Prince of Wales – later to become King George V.

1919 was the first summer that Kitty 'went public'. Although she had played in only four tournaments before the championships, which were held at the end of June, she had already shown enough promise for her entry to be accepted by the All England club. It must have felt very like school again. She was the promising new girl who had reached two quarter finals, one semi final and who had won the doubles final at the Gipsy Club in North London with Miss Holman. In her opening four tournaments she had taken nine games off the experienced senior player, Elizabeth Ryan, taking her to an 8–6 second set. That must have raised a few eyebrows.

This was the background to her first championship. With all Worple Road watching inquisitively, Kitty reached the quarter final only to find herself drawn against the dazzling new French champion Suzanne Lenglen. It was cruel luck to be required to face such a task and she duly lost 6–0, 6–1.

When Kitty first entered the ladies singles in 1919, there were forty-four competitors. From 1900 up to 1914 the entry had varied between seventeen and fifty-two. From 1919 to 1930 the numbers rose gradually from 44 to 51, 57, 64, 70, 64 in 1924, 25 and 26, to 80 the next two years and to 96 in 1929 and 1930. These days the ladies singles entry is 128.

Today the choice of entry and the seeding of players is largely directed by computer placings; these placings are calculated from results all over the world. In Kitty's day a player would apply to the All-England committee for an entry form. Filled in with the necessary information and results of domestic tournaments, this would be judged by the entry selection committee. If accepted the cost would be thirty shillings – ten shillings each if you played in the singles, doubles and mixed doubles.

Tennis fashion changed during the days of the All-England championships at Worple Road. Initially the whites tended to be rather starchy but quickly the players adopted looser, freer clothing. Suzanne Lenglen's arrival marked the virtual end of ankle length skirts for women players – and with the new calf-length skirts came more loosely cut blouses.

So this was Worple Road in the years just before and after the 1914–18 war. A few years ago Kitty's son David received a Christmas card of an aerial photograph of Worple Road. He disguised it before showing it to his mother but, in an instant, Kitty recognised it. She put her finger on one of the courts saying: 'That's where Suzanne beat me 6–0, 6–1.' That was her first taste of Lenglen, and the experience must have made a lasting impression. Even after an interval of sixty years it was a case of instant recall.

It was in that same summer of 1919 that another notable visit was made to the club when King George V and Queen Mary twice visited the championships. As if to do them due honour the official programme was printed on paper instead of cardboard, with the price raised from six pence to one shilling. Because of rain the meeting was extended to a third Tuesday, though that did not prevent all five championships being won by overseas players for the first time.

It was in the very next year, 1920, that rumours began to circulate that there was a move afoot. The committee wished to enlarge the Worple Road grounds but their efforts to rent or purchase adjoining properties had failed. The owners of one field who would not sell wanted £500 rent for the two weeks of the championships. But the committee were far-seeing. In 1920 they recognised that parking space for motor cars was becoming a problem. Instead of accepting the situation as it was they began to investigate the possibility of moving lock, stock and barrel to the Park Road, later Church Road, site.

Meanwhile, on the playing side in 1920, two of the best players in the world were to decorate Worple Road. Only the previous summer

Suzanne Lenglen had won the first of her six singles titles, and she now returned. And from America there came long and lean Bill Tilden, who not only took the men's title, but was to go into history as probably the greatest of all men players. The same might also be said of Suzanne Lenglen amongst the women – but these judgements survive as opinions that can never be proved, although interestingly Lenglen, that same summer, became the first competitor to win the three titles of singles, doubles and mixed doubles.

The decision to move was eventually taken with the actual changeover taking place in 1922. The modern, more extensive Wimbledon site was prepared and the construction of a huge new centre court was initiated.

Though Kitty may not have felt any pang of sorrow for the transfer there was, nonetheless, forty-four years of history and growth behind dear old Worple Road. To some it must have felt like the retirement of some long-serving faithful servant. But Tilden and Lenglen did their duty by bowing out, each with their titles, as a fond farewell, and Suzanne for one left her mark on Worple Road by playing the last ever stroke on the centre court of the old place.

It was both a watershed and an historic moment when Wimbledon was opened in 1922. Great events lay ahead. In the coming years there was to unfold a vast change to tennis – not only in its playing but with a rise in overall standards. There was also to be a change in the players themselves with a related and subtle shift in social standards.

The new ground of thirteen and a half acres, three times the size of Worple Road, was officially opened on June 26, 1922, at a cost of £146,000. In the meantime the ten courts and two freehold residences of Worple Road were put up for sale.

At Wimbledon the new centre court was built of reinforced concrete. Three thousand tons of shingle, 1700 tons of sand and 600 tons of cement were used. The turf was brought from Cumberland, as was used for the pitch at Wembley Stadium which was opened in the following year in time for the Football Association Cup Final. The stands and court were positioned so that no shadow could appear until seven o'clock in the evening and a small disc of white paper, placed on the turf, could be seen from every seat. Courts No 1 and No 2 were not erected until later and at the opening Wimbledon had twelve courts beside the new centre court. At the beginning admission to the ground was three shillings and six pence, and there were parking facilities for 400 cars.

King George V and Queen Mary – the latter a frequent visitor in the years ahead – arrived for the opening. Sadly, rain interfered and the scheduled 2.00 pm start was delayed. Eventually, however, the King appeared in the royal box at 3.30 pm, gave three blows on a gong and declared the new grounds open. At that the centre court tarpaulin was removed and the first match was played between A R F Kingscote and L A Godfree, the man later to be Kitty's husband.

The players had previously agreed to show their respects to their King and Queen, so, walking towards the umpire's chair they stopped half-way, about turned and bowed graciously towards the royal box. Thus a tradition was born that is still followed today by all the players who perform before royalty on the centre court.

L A Godfree won the toss and chose to serve. As the two players were having their customary knock-up, Godfree decided that, as this was the very first match on the new centre court, he wanted to 'pocket' the first ball as a keepsake.

When the umpire called the players to order, so that the match could start, Godfree served the first ball into the bottom of the net and ran like a hare to retrieve it. But it turned out to be a real race, as Kingscote had exactly the same idea, so there was a picture of two men rushing to the net with but a single aim – Godfree got there first!

Unfortunately the balls in those days were rubber based with a wool covering and hand-stitched. As the years went by, the moths attacked the wool and the rubber started to perish and some forty years on the remains of that ball had to be disposed of by Kitty – a small but sad tale.

Intermittent showers spoiled the rest of the afternoon so that there was no play on any of the outer courts and only one gentlemen's doubles completed on what was a disappointing afternoon spoiled by English weather. In fact it was worse than that. Those who grumble these days at inclement Wimbledon weather may wish to know that the opening of the Club's bright new ground was extended to the third Wednesday of the fortnight – to July 12 – because of rain interference on every day of the meeting. But one important decision was taken by the committee at that stage. It was decided to abolish the Challenge Round of the gentlemen's and ladies' singles and the gentlemen's doubles, which meant that future reigning champions would be put on their mettle.

Two years later courts No 1 and No 2 were added to the complex which brought the total to fifteen including the centre court. In 1924 a simple form of seeding was tried and in the following year a qualifying competition was established, held at Roehampton, allowing eight singles winners and four doubles pairs to join the main championship – a reflection of the growth of prospective entries.

Apart from other alterations and improvements – including an added twenty-seven seats for the press box – the big event of 1926 was the fiftieth birthday of the Championships, a jubilee celebration attended by King George V and Queen Mary.

For a change the weather did not interfere as thirty-four ex-champions of the men's singles and doubles and ladies' singles paraded on the centre court to be presented to their Majesties. Each champion received a silver commemorative medal while all the rest of the competitors received a bronze medal.

While all the champions on the centre court parade were smartly dressed in suits and dresses, four of that company were noticed to be wearing tennis attire. This was done to save time.

The reason for this was that following the presentation an exhibition ladies' doubles match of one set was organised, played between Suzanne Lenglen and Elizabeth Ryan, winners for six of the previous seven years, and Kitty and Miss Kea Bouman, a Dutch girl. As the score grew from 4-all and 5-all to 6-all, the excited crowd changed the mood of an exhibition into a challenge match. The loud cheering clearly supported Kitty and her partner against such supreme opposition. When Kitty and Bouman eventually won 8–6 the wild cheering might have indicated that they were the world champions. It was a wonderful moment. And to make it a royal occasion the left-handed Duke of York – later King George VI – partnered Group Captain Sir Louis Greig (later Chairman of the Club) in the men's doubles event.

After Kitty and partner had 'won' the exhibition match, a member, sitting in the member's stand quietly said to Leslie Godfree 'that will cause a furore as Suzanne never likes being beaten'. Shortly after that exhibition she withdrew from the tournament.

Full seeding eventually came into operation in 1927 in a year when a fifteen year old American, S B ('Boy') Wood shocked the centre court crowd by appearing in the holy of holies in white plus-fours and golfing stockings. Four years later, seeded No 7, he won the singles title by a walkover against another American, F X Shields, who had injured himself in the semi final. It was also the year when the first radio broadcast took place from the centre court. Wimbledon was being dragged into the twentieth century.

The Club has seldom allowed the grass to grow under its feet. Nearly every year there have been improvements and alterations to meet both the accommodation needs of the growing crowds and the comfort of the competitors and working officials. At the same time efforts have been made to maintain the event as a friendly and mannerly social gathering.

The rules about the attire of players have always been carefully guarded, particularly in matters of colours. Players must wear predominantly white. The reaction of the committee will be interesting if, and when, coloured balls are suggested. As for clothing worn during the championship there were the golfing plus-fours of 'Boy' Wood in the 1920s, the shorts of Bunny Austin in the 1930s and the last of the traditional long white flannels just after the second war worn by Yvon Petra of France. For the ladies in 1927 Miss Billie Tapscott took to a court without stockings as an expression of freedom; Miss Ryan took out the bones of her stays on a very hot day in 1921 and georgeous 'Gussie' Moran daringly wore Teddy Tinling's coloured lace panties in the 1950s.

The growing popularity of the event was reflected in 1932 when over 200,000 spectators attended the fortnight. Only fifty-five years earlier a mere 200 had attended the opening final!

Ten years after the arrival of radio, in 1927, on the centre court there now followed BBC television to meet the level of interest in the country. Nowadays Wimbledon television broadcasts fill many hours of the day.

But before the days of televised matches, in 1934, had come a double British triumph, the first since 1908. F J Perry and Miss Dorothy Round won the gentlemen's and ladies' singles. The All-England committee were so elated by this that a suggestion was made that Miss Round should be elected as an honorary member. But opposition to this came from one quarter. Why, came the question, should four other surviving earlier champions be ignored – Lottie Dod, Mrs Sterry, Mrs Chambers and Kitty Godfree? The committee bowed to this. So a distinguished quartet all became honorary members, Kitty ten years after her 1924 win over Helen Wills.

The advent of the second world war put a stop to everything from 1940 to 1945. On the revival in 1946 Wimbledon looked little changed from 1939 except that a 500lb bomb had fallen on the roof of the centre court in October 1940 and thus denied spectators of 1200 seats. But as building restrictions gradually eased repairs were undertaken to the centre court and the lost places restored.

Once a year the royal box is, at the invitation of the Club officials, a meeting place of visitors, diplomats, parliamentarians and the peerage. When royal visitors arrive they are escorted to chairs of a padded variety, provided with rugs, footstools and programmes, and later tea and strawberries in adjacent rooms. In the days of Queen Mary many of the other guests would receive friendly little nods. The Queen was a keen follower of the game and was noted for wearing blue smoked glasses on her Wimbledon visits.

On one occasion King George V was deep in conversation with George Hillyard. As he lingered the Queen, who was waiting in the entrance, was heard to call out, like any other wife: 'Oh, come on George we'll be late for dinner.' On one of Queen Mary's last appearances at Wimbledon she remarked to Lieutenant Colonel Duncan Macaulay, Secretary of the Club, that she probably would not come again since the stairs were proving too much for her to negotiate. To which he replied: 'Ma'am, we can surely put in an escalator.' Sadly it was not needed.

Queen Elizabeth II has not inherited the same interest in the game as her grandmother. The royal family of today care more for horses, horse racing, show jumping and polo. However, she has attended Wimbledon on three or four occasions and was present when Althea Gibson, of the United States, became the first black player to become a champion.

In 1908 Mrs Sterry, five times the ladies' champion at the turn of the century, wrote: 'To my idea nothing looks smarter, and more in keeping with the game of tennis than a nice hanging white skirt, about two inches off the ground, white blouse, white band and pale coloured silk tie and white collar.' But the years slipped by. First there was Suzanne Lenglen and later Mr Teddy Tinling as the charm of that gentle fashionable Edwardian age vanished.

With its passing has come a revolution in the game. Behind the scenes lurk publicity and literary agents, managers and coaches, advertising sharks, so that it can be said that the modern player is wrapped in cotton wool. Today's champions have become like protected animals. The money prizes today are enormous – six figures now where once, only sixty years ago, it was a £5 voucher for Mappin and Webb merchandise.

The modern players arrive for the championship in fleets of courtesy cars from their four or five star hotels – no more walking from stations carrying kit or travelling in buses. This is twentieth century showbiz treatment.

Kitty herself, as an ex-champion, is entitled to an occasional courtesy car when invited to a Wimbledon reception party and indeed was provided with one when invited to a Buckingham Palace tea party three or four years ago. She went with her son David but forgot to take the invitation. The two of them were escorted straight to the Lord Chamberlain's office at the far side of the inner quadrangle, where the matter was put right. 'A good way to beat the queue!' said the lady attendant with a smile as she pointed them towards the tea lawns.

Every summer Wimbledon receives a vast amount of free publicity from the media. Perhaps in recognition of this the All-England committee has listened to most demands by the press. Three times in the past fifteen years they have increased the comfort and size of the journalists' writing rooms as well as the refreshment restaurant, bars and telephone facilities.

In 1985, for instance, £4 million were spent on the latest expansion. Symbolically, perhaps, a giant thunder storm struck on the opening day when a streak of forked lightning bit off lumps of masonry from the new roof. On another afternoon a rainstorm of monsoon proportions flooded the courts; young people were seen swimming in the passageways beneath the centre court. However, the tarpaulin tents on the centre and No 1 courts saved the day's play as they held the rain at bay.

In 1977, the centenary of the championships, the Wimbledon lawn tennis museum and library was opened. In this matter considerable help was given by Mr Tom Todd, a great enthusiast, who had retired to the Channel Islands where he had set up his private museum of tennis memorabilia. He graciously transferred this to Wimbledon to help establish an official, public museum of days past. It is here that a painting of Kitty in tennis attire is to be seen.

The All-England Club gave an example to the tennis world in 1968 by promoting the first professional championship, a step which brought honesty to what previously had become a game of shamateurs. The idea for this came from Herman David in 1958, at a special general meeting when he was Chairman – but it took ten years to materialise.

In 1977 Queen Elizabeth II attended the championships when the Club celebrated its centenary. Again there came a parade of surviving men and women singles champions on the centre court when each player was presented with a commemorative medal by the Duke and Duchess of Kent. The Duke has been President of the Club since 1969. Kitty, as the oldest surviving champion, was the last in the queue for presentation.

In 1984 there came a centenary of the ladies' championship (begun in 1884) when the survivors each received a handsome cut glass crystal vase. In 1986 followed a centenary of actual play since 1877, the difference on the calendar explained by the lost years of two wars.

In 1931 wrought iron memorial gates were erected at the Church Road entrance (East) in honour of the Doherty brothers who were winners many times, around the 1890s. In 1984 the west entrance gates were named after Fred Perry as a reminder of his three consecutive singles wins fifty years earlier. There is also a full length statue of him near the tea lawns which was unveiled by the Duke of Kent on a special day in 1984, together with a small bronze 'action' statue of Kitty which now resides in the members' lounge.

It is outside these same Fred Perry gates that long queues of hardy fans sprawl out on the pavements, many of them having spent the night in the open, regardless of the weather. Once inside the gates there is usually a scramble for standing places. To stake out an early claim there are those who develop a serpentine craftiness.

Wimbledon has the power to stir up something more than excitement. Even in the rain the place has a grandeur, a sense of antiquity, an air of tradition. Good humour abounds because the fortnight represents to both young and old an escape from the world and its problems. To both it remains something of a pageant.

And although styles change and, perhaps, Wimbledon has lost some of its elegance there are still feasts and junketings on the enclosed sacrosanct members' lawn. Here some tables are red with wine and roses – yet there is a sadness. A secret sorrow lurks; it is the memory of the departed friends who, for so long, came to the annual meeting. But, of course, this is a temple only for the dignitaries who sport the purple and dark green All-England Club ties. Wimbledon's inner circle still aims for the elitist.

Most spectators have to be content with merely feasting the eye on window boxes of formal flowers and on clumps of glistening hydrangea; whole awnings of luminous colour that garnish the grey setting and even defy the weather.

Wimbledon is theatre. The players are the actors. The court is the stage, a setting for a play sometimes of dramatic content and sometimes soporific. The actors each strive for a star part or a moment of glory, all caught in the bright footlights, all affected by the smell of the grease paint and the roar of the crowd. Many dreams are shattered early but who would deny the right to dream?

6

W i m b l e d o n   W i n n i n g
F i n a l s — 1 9 2 4   a n d   1 9 2 6

It is obviously difficult, if not impossible, for Kitty to remember details of her Wimbledon final matches. They return only as brush strokes on a broad canvas. Let me underline this by saying that she had complete-ly forgotten that she was in the final of 1923 when Lenglen beat her by 6–2, 6–2.

'Good Lord', she said, 'I didn't realise that, was I *really* in the final? Jolly good!' The reason for this blank probably was that her victory the very next year erased the memory: either that or Suzanne finished the match so quickly that no imprint remains.

However, she does recall some of that 1924 triumph when she beat Helen Wills 4–6, 6–4, 6–4. These are her words. They emerge through the mists of the past.

'It was very nerve-wracking, walking on to the centre court that July afternoon, watched by the Queen. The crowds naturally were in support of an English player, but I was not too confident of winning even though I had beaten Helen in the Wightman Cup only a week earlier. I knew that Helen was a fine young player and a hard hitter who would be keen to get her revenge.

'I had a reputation for being a strong finisher. But equally true was the fact that I was a weak starter. So it proved. Helen took the first set 6–4 after I had led 3–1. I dissipated that start as Helen took nine out of the next eleven games. She led by 4–1 and 40–15 in the second set. It looked all over.

'The crowd still tried to back me up but I knew at that point I'd have to change my tactics to keep alive. Helen was winning with storming drives down both wings and I decided my one hope was to attack. I began to produce one or two good length drives of my own which took me to the net to volley any returns. With a couple of net cords the luck began to turn my way and I saved that sixth game from 15–40 and instead of 1–5 the score became 2–4, an important difference.

'Now it became ding-dong, as the crowd, sensing a change in the tide, reached a pitch of excitement. Before I knew it I had taken that set from nowhere and the match was level. At this stage I felt that Helen had begun to worry, wondering what had happened, as is often the case when a lead begins to slip away.

'The crowd, of course, lifted me in a tight final set as I saw it out at 6–4. The cheering was overwhelming as this was the first English victory since Mrs Lambert Chambers had won before the first war in 1914. A gap of ten years had now been filled.

'Helen was very sporting in defeat as we shook hands and thanked each other; we then shook hands with the umpire, collected our sweaters and left the court to ringing cheers.

'In those days there was no finishing ceremony as now, no royalty to present a prize on the court, no parade of linesmen, umpire or referee, no avenue of ballboys for a royal entrance and no bouquets. No. All we did was collect our things from the umpire's steps and leave for a bath and a cup of tea which I had with my mother and father in the members enclosure. What we received was a voucher for £5 – from the All-England Club, through the post a few days later, on Mappin & Webb, the jewellers. We didn't miss any formal ceremony because in those days there was none.'

All one need add is that Kitty entered like the proverbial lamb but went out like a lioness. That, she now says, was her finest match against an opponent who never lost again at Wimbledon. But in the dressing room later a doctor had to attend a burst and bleeding blister on 'Wills' foot.

Here follow two match reports of the 1924 final as seen through the critical eyes of Suzanne Lenglen on behalf of the *Daily Express* and Wallis Myers for the *Daily Telegraph*:

MISS McKANE TENNIS CHAMPION

by Suzanne Lenglen (Specially written for the *Daily Express*).

In a match which was an exciting spectacle but not great lawn tennis, Miss Kitty McKane regained for Britain the women's championship at Wimbledon yesterday by beating Miss Helen Wills, the champion of America, by 2 sets to 1.

Both girls appeared to feel the strain of the situation.

Miss Wills was outwardly as perfectly calm as usual, but her strokes were not altogether under control. Miss McKane was obviously unable to find her touch. The first game went to Miss Wills, who was serving, with only one point to Miss McKane. The next three were all love games to Miss McKane. Miss Wills lost her service without an ace to her credit.

But with the fifth game goodness came to both. They began to drive and to volley and to serve with more snap.

When Miss Wills was 4–3 there was a great struggle. Miss McKane was at 0–40. It seemed hopeless for her.

She brought off a splendid cross-drive and gained the next three points.

Deuce. But see, another double fault. Miss Wills has the advantage. She loses it with a weak forehand which goes into the net. She hits out. Miss McKane has made it four-all.

There was a grand game to follow. Both girls urged to supreme effort, contested it point by point. Miss Wills finessed for the net and hit harder. Miss McKane used the tactics of care. But Miss Wills, with a delightful drop volley and some shrewd use of the court, outplayed her opponent.

This phase continued in the next game, and Miss Wills won the first set at 6–4.

The impression people had was that Miss McKane would have to play much better to win the match. The necessary 'pep' was wanting.

With the first game of the second set Miss McKane seemed to be going to wake up, but she lapsed. It went to 4–1 against her.

'All is over!' they were saying. 'It is not Miss McKane. Where is she?'

But this is the point where the English girl is so wonderful, where the grit of her country shows in her.

Mark what happened. With the sixth game of the second set, it was a new Miss McKane. A girl who sprang to the stroke, who sprang to the net, who made the ball travel on her famous forehand-drive like the way it does from a cricket bat.

Miss Wills put up a stout resistance, but the effect of the powerful attack was to make her begin to lose her accuracy.

Her Little 'Hanky'

I do not think that she quite realised what was happening. So swiftly did she lose the next five games, the last one to love on Miss McKane's service, that the set was gone from her as you take a cake from a plate when one who wanted it is looking the other way.

In appearance Miss Wills was the only unperturbed person on the ground.

She moved the same, she looked the same. At no greater or less speed and with no different a gesture did she continue to take her little 'hanky' from her little breast pocket, and with it dabbed either her eyes, precisely – or her nose, precisely.

Such a battle there was for the first four games of the third set. Miss McKane won the first, making her series six.

The pace she had set was telling upon her. At two games all she leaned upon her racket. Service was rather an effort.

But she did not slacken in the least. She dare not. Miss Wills became better, and produced some 'peaches' of passes but, in reply, so did Miss McKane. Royalty were in the box, and it was a battle royal.

When it came to 4–3 against her, Miss Wills was serving. The score was 15–30 against her, when Miss McKane got a very lucky net, which made the score 15–40. With one of her typical forehand drives Miss McKane finished off the game. So it was 4–4. Miss McKane then went on to win the set and the match.

I was impressed by the improvement Miss Wills exhibited. She played much better than I had thought she could from what I had seen her do before. When she begins to alter her game more to fit in with conditions her fine stroke production will make her a much greater player.

THRILLING FINAL AT WIMBLEDON

by A Wallis Myers CBE

American Independence Day, the anniversary of McLoughlin's great bid for the Single Championship against Tony Wilding, and the stage set for another Californian quest – this time on the Ladies' Singles Championship. And the attributes of a great occasion were there. The sun was shining, the centre court was packed as it had never been packed before this year, the Queen (and with her the Duke and Duchess of York) was in the Royal box. Commander Hillyard was in his accustomed place (in the final) on the umpire's chair; the lines were held by distinguished players. All the day demanded was a great match. This desideratum, at first denied, was supplied. At the end of an hour and a quarter's play Miss McKane had beaten Miss Helen Wills by two sets to one, each set having yielded ten games.

But what an agony of suspense and fluctuation before the championship point was scored. What a match for both ladies to dream about. What a brilliant break of all court play which carried the American champion three times within a stroke of 5–1 in the second set – a lead which, had it been secured, must almost inevitably have given her the British championship as well! What a wonderful recovery of Miss McKane, who, when all seemed lost, captured six games in succession and tipped the scales in her favour! Finally, what a thrilling final set, with every stroke of vital value, with neither player 'rattled' yet straining every nerve for victory, with Miss Wills twice needing only a point for a 4–2 lead, and with Miss McKane determined she should not get it, with each country dead level at 4-all, and with England, drawing on a deeper experience, just winning in the end.

Play of High Quality

Let me emphasise that the play, except in the early phase, when Miss Wills lost twelve successive points, was of a remarkably high standard. I doubt whether any Lenglen match at Wimbledon (except the first in 1919) has provided rallies so keenly contested or strokes of such resource, variety and skill. Helen Wills was as near her American best as I have ever seen her; she redeemed every estimate of her stroke equipment, speed, and accuracy formed on the other side; save in her judgement on two or three occasions, when she returned balls that were going out of court, she revealed all the qualities of a champion. She flouted the notion that she could not move quickly over the court; she confounded those who imagined that her form in the international match was her true form, just as much as those who believed, after her championship matches at Wimbledon, that she could not hit a hard ball to the right place. If you ask why, with all these virtues, and with the commanding lead which they brought her, she did not win, the answer must be that Miss McKane's volleys in the last set, especially towards its close, were more incisive than her own. When the soul-searching came to its crisis, when each player had been moved from a winning position into a losing position by the enterprise of the other, when the good lob had been recovered or the low cross drive countered, when the advance for the kill finally undertaken and the opportunity to make it was offered, it was Miss McKane who, with her longer experience of net play, stowed away the ball to a spot from which it never returned. Miss Wills made beautiful volleys; more polished in their lustre, some of them were, than the volleys of Miss McKane. I recollect one deep smash in the third set which McLoughlin could not have bettered. But the tendency was there, and it had a material effect in the last set, to chop the volley rather than to hit it with a plain faced racket, as Miss McKane hits it.

The Match in Retrospect

I come to the match in brief survey. Miss Wills, serving, took the opening game without a challenge. She lost the next three, offering none herself. Three love games to Miss McKane. The wiseacres all began to talk at once. The struggle had not yet begun. Miss Wills took the fifth game from 15, the sixth from 30, and the seventh from 15. She had found her drive, both forehand and back; Miss McKane's had temporarily left her – there was an increasing lack of control under pressure. It seemed certain Miss Wills could go to 5–3 when she was offered, at short range, an easy drive past a volleyer; but she hit the ball too softly, her opponent moved over and intercepted; there followed a tremendous fight for the eighth game. Miss McKane won it in spite of three double faults. A great rally opened the ninth game; the crowd went almost delirious; but Miss Wills had now begun an invincible phase, and she took the first set unfalteringly and with increasing speed at 6–4.

Without serious check, and with wonderful composure, she advanced to 4–1 in the second set. She kept Miss McKane away from the net by perfect lobbing; she hit the chalk with her cross-drives, she used her powerful backhand drive down the line; she was as sound in defence as in attack. The odds on her winning at this stage were something like six to one. Then came the palpitating conflict for the sixth game. Three times the American was within a stroke of it; but she had no easy chance; indeed, Miss McKane made two of her finest forehand drives to get up to vantage. But its fate virtually decided this set. Miss Wills was never within call of the next three games. Miss McKane took the tenth game to love. She had found new strength in adversity; her forcing drive was operating at its best; the complementary volleys fitted in. Miss Wills saw her great lead wiped out.

They were dead level at 2–2 in the final set. The pace had dropped a little under the physical strain; it only came back to its maximum when the tussle for the sixth game was waged. Three-all, instead of 4–2 for Miss Wills. Miss McKane's splendid cross-drives and two volleying errors by her opponent carried her to 4–3, and then to 5–3. Could she be caught now? Miss Wills evidently thought so, for she served brilliantly in the ninth game, and won it with this offensive weapon alone. Thirty-love and then thirty-all in the next game; forty-thirty after a tense rally. Then a silence that could almost be felt. Miss Wills attempts a low back-hand drive off her body; it hits the band; Miss McKane is champion; the crowds acclaim – and the tea enclosures are choked. One final, and perhaps the most dramatic, was over.

The New Champion

The new lady champion, a native of London, is the first English title-holder since 1914. The reign of France was broken, perhaps only temporarily, by the retirement of Mlle Lenglen, after five years' regality. Suzanne had won the hard court championship of the world in Paris before the war, when she was a child of 13. Miss Kathleen McKane did not come to fame until after the war, and she differs fundamentally from the French girl in that she had no coach to fashion either her strokes or her tactics. She is a self-made player, and an example and inspiration to all girls who, whatever their opportunity for practice, can push their way to the front by individual effort. She was one of many zealous, athletic English girls, adept at golf and Badminton (of which she is the present champion), riding horses and sleigh with equal relish, who threw themselves as eagerly into war work as into peace play. I remember seeing her first play in 1919 at Chiswick Park – a pretty, merry volleyer, with a long vaulting stride, a natural hitter if there ever was one. She did not wear, and has never worn, the solemn mien of some players of her sex, and doubtless it has been this air of joyous abandon, index of an unaffected nature, which has made her so popular with crowds wherever she has played.

Despite the glowing reports Kitty is more modest in her assessment of her first and most famous championship victory.

'Having beaten Helen in the Wightman Cup just before Wimbledon I felt she would be all out for revenge. Having no job at that time I had time for practice between the championship rounds, but that was the usual habit. There was no special training; it came naturally as the matches progressed, with a thankful break at the semi final when I should have faced Suzanne Lenglen who had scratched. We did not like to leave our fitness on a practice court.

'When I faced Helen in the final I don't think I had worked out any special tactical plan. If I remember I think I played it as it came, knowing that Helen hit hard to a fine length. It was only when on the brink of defeat in the second set – 4-1 down that I started to match Helen's driving and at least having found a length myself, started to dominate the net. Earlier I believe I had advanced on a bad length which allowed the American to pass me on each flank.

'Since the rule of a match said that "play shall be continuous", Commander Hillyard, the annual umpire for the ladies' final, allowed little leeway at the change of ends. Seats for rest for the contestants to towel down, drink and even change shirts did not exist in those days. All Commander Hillyard allowed was a quick drink at the foot of the umpire's steps. There was litle wastage of time so that even a long three set match took little more than an hour to finish.

'Helen Wills in 1924 was a rather shy; quiet teenager on her first visit to Europe. I was some ten years the older, on my home ground, and was naturally the more mature. But we liked and respected each other and there was little of the fierce rivarly that is sometimes to be found today. Indeed, it was a hard but friendly match. Yet little did I realise that Helen was never to be beaten again in the championship.

Never at any time did I think I was destined to be champion. In fact I don't suppose I ever should have achieved that position had not Suzanne Lenglen scratched in the two years I took the title. She was too good for me and for everybody else as well. I knew it and accepted it. If there is a parallel today it must surely be Martina Navratilova.'

The year after the victory over Wills, Kitty received a 6–0, 6–0 drubbing by Lenglen in the semi final. Thus Kitty's one object in 1926 was to repair her loss of face for that cruel beating the previous summer. Lenglen attended Wimbledon in 1926, but withdrew from all events after reaching the third round of the singles. In fact, she never played there again, turning professional late in 1926. She signed for the American CC Pyle, and toured America from October 1926 to February 1927.

With Lenglen thus withdrawn Kitty again won through to the final. Unfortunately the match against Senorita Lili de Alvarez, the Spanish champion, lacked the fire of the Wills battle. Certainly Kitty again finished strongly but the match as a whole was much less gritty against a carefree, elegant opponent.

At a set-all, Kitty trailed 1–3 in the decider. Alvarez was then showing her true colours. While Kitty concentrated on avoiding mistakes Lili revealed all her Spanish flair with some fine tennis. Yet once more the lioness of Kitty began to roar. Taking the last five games in succession she ran out the winner by 6–2, 4–6, 6–3.

That year, 1926, was a happy one for Kitty. First she got married to Leslie Godfree. Then, though America took the Wightman Cup by four matches to three, Kitty won both her singles, beating Mary Browne and Elizabeth Ryan. She regained the Wimbledon singles title, won the mixed doubles championship with husband Leslie, and reached the finals of the women's doubles.

That was not a bad catch for a summer remembering also that Kitty had taken the last eleven games in her semi final against Mlle Vlasto of France that year to win 6–4, 6–0.

7

The Wightman Cup

Women's tennis in England is on a slightly higher plane at this time than in America; but the standard of play in America is rapidly coming up. International competition between women on the lines of the Davis Cup, for which a trophy has previously been offered by Lady Wavertree in England, and in 1919 by Mrs Wightman in America, and thrice refused by the International Federation, would do more than any other factor to place women's tennis on the high plane desired. This plan has succeeded for the men, why should it not do as well for the women?

Looking at Tilden's 1921 views of women's tennis it is fascinating to note that he saw the need for growth in international competition; he also hinted at the possible start of the now famous Wightman Cup. In our time, of course, there has been added the Federation Cup involving several nations.

It was in 1922 that Mrs Wightman got her way, thus adding American sponsorship to another international competition. In reply Great Britain at once answered the challenge through the Lawn Tennis Association and in 1923 became the first sporting governing body to send a women's team overseas officially.

It was a new chapter in tennis history. The team chosen was Mrs Phyllis Covell, Kitty, Mrs Mabel Clayton, and Mrs Geraldine Beamish, with Humbert Sabelli, the Lawn Tennis Association secretary as non-playing captain and manager.

On July 22 the party boarded the *SS Franconia* at Liverpool and were due to land at New York in a week. Unfortunately because of immigration difficulties, they did not get their land legs until August 1. They were due to fulfil a fixture at Seabright, New Jersey, but decided to withdraw. The hosts, however, were so persuasive they talked the British party into playing after all.

Kitty, with no practice, reached the semi final where she lost in blazing heat to Mrs Mallory. But she won the doubles with Mrs Covell, who became one of her regular partners.

The tournament over, the British women moved back to New York for some late practice before the opening of the historic tie at Forest Hills at the West Side Club. That was the beginning of the Wightman Cup.

After a short ceremony Forest Hills was baptised and the contest began. Kitty opened with a match against the seventeen year old Helen Wills; Miss Wills was due to become the new American champion in a week's time. With this match Kitty had the distinction of playing the first match of the first Wightman Cup.

On a strange court, in a bustling new city, with strange food, the party did not settle down comfortably. Indeed they lost every match in a fixture that was due to be played on Friday and Saturday, August 10 and 11, but was rearranged to Saturday and Monday August 11 and 13 because of the funeral of President Harding.

A defeat by 7–0 was hard to bear but the simple fact was the British team played below their true ability in strange conditions while the Americans were in top form. Kitty lost to Helen Willis 2–6, 5–7 and to Mrs Mallory 2–6, 3–6. She went down in the doubles, too, with Mrs Covell to Mrs Hazel Wightman and Miss Goss by 8–10, 7–5, 4–6. In fact, Kitty missed a set point against Wills. Having been outplayed in the opening she actually led 5–2, 40–15 in the second set before being caught and passed. But a year later there would be sweet revenge.

Meanwhile when the American championships arrived a week later the British began to show some form. Kitty lost again to Wills in the quarter finals but this time succeeded to capture the first set in a score of 6–2, 2–6, 5–7. Then she and Mrs Covell avenged their Wightman Cup doubles defeat by winning the national title against Mrs Wightman and Miss Goss 2–6, 6–2, 6–1. Kitty also reached the mixed final with Jack Hawkes, the Australian, but lost to the powerful partnership of Tilden and Mrs Mallory. After the sad start at Forest Hills this was a reasonable recovery.

Serious competition over for a while there came a few days of sightseeing and shopping amidst the skyscrapers of New York before taking the train to Canada via the Niagara Falls. The Canadians met them with great warmth and friendship as they arranged a series of matches and exhibitions at Toronto, Ottawa, Montreal and Quebec. Having enjoyed their trip and learned much in the process the party set back for England on the *SS Empress of France* on September 15, having spent two months away from home.

While women players of today fly from country to country and are constantly on the go, that first British party tasted something new and, being comparatively unsophisticated, found it all very strange. Although thoroughly whitewashed in the Wightman Cup the experience proved invaluable as was proved when the Americans came to England in the June of 1924.

In the second Wightman Cup, this time played at Wimbledon just before the championships in June, Britain swept the Americans aside by six matches to one, the Americans themselves feeling uncomfortable on their first visit to England. Kitty won both her singles this time, beating Mrs Mallory 6–3, 6–3, and Helen Wills, the new champion of the United States, by 6–2, 6–2. Kitty, however, with a fresh partner, Evelyn Colyer, lost a doubles to Mrs Wightman and Wills by 6–2, 2–6, 4–6.

Here is a list of Wightman Cup matches in which Kitty took part:

At Forest Hills	1923	–	USA 7	GB 0	(Kitty singles and doubles)	
At Wimbledon	1924	–	USA 1	GB 6	('' '' '' ''	)
At Forest Hills	1925	–	USA 3	GB 4	('' '' '' ''	)
At Wimbledon	1926	–	USA 4	GB 3	('' '' '' ''	)
At Forest Hills	1927	–	USA 5	GB 2	('' '' '' ''	)
At Wimbledon	1928	)	Kitty did not play;			
At Forest Hills	1929	)	birth of first son.			
At Wimbledon	1930	–	USA 3	GB 4	) Kitty only played	
At Wimbledon	1934	–	USA 5	GB 2	) doubles	

Kitty's total: Singles – Won 5, Lost 5.
                  Doubles – Won 2, Lost 5.

Of these the British victory at Forest Hills in 1925 – one of the few 'away' wins in a long list of American triumphs over the years – is perhaps of interest. Here follows an official report reproduced by the team manager, Mr J Arthur Batley. It was significant that on this occasion the less important trip to Canada was made before the challenge of America was undertaken, unlike the visit in 1923. This change of plan paid dividends.

August 1 2

A cable from the authorities at home gave us permission to remain until the 31st inst. so as to take part in the Mixed Doubles championships at Longwood, Boston, on the 26th, so we altered our arrangements accordingly.

Mr A Wallis-Myers and Mr R Powell-Blackmore arrived from England today, so we should have at least two 'fans' among the crowd next Friday.

Laundry work is just as scandalously expensive and bad, in New York as it was in Canada, and is a serious handicap to cleanliness. That the ladies of the party should again be driven to doing some of their own washing may sound amusing, but it was a case of real necessity, and they were good enough to help the men out too.

We lunched at the Tennis Club Forest Hills and again had some very good practice on the gallery courts.

At four o'clock the second trial match between Bill Johnston and Vince Richards was staged for the right to play second string in the Davis Cup Team. The first was played last Saturday when Johnston won by 9–7 in the fifth set after a most brilliant and punishing contest. Today 'Little Bill' was master of the situation throughout and won in three straight sets, after a magnificent display of all-round tennis, and thus well earned the right to a place in the team.

In the evening we were the honoured guests at a dinner-dance given by the West Side Lawn Tennis Club at the Vanderbilt Hotel, and it was one of the jolliest and most successful functions imaginable. There were about fifty people present, including the American Ladies Team which we were to meet on Friday, and many other well-known men and ladies in the tennis world. We had a most excellent dinner, and 'Scotch' was readily forthcoming for those who wanted it, although the Steward from the Club had to be present to handle it. What a farce! Those who 'wanted' seemed to be in the majority, and I found it difficult to make anyone believe that I did not take it. The reply invariably came back: 'What! an Englishman, and not drink whisky?' You see the reputation we have abroad! In England I suppose we should say – 'What! an American, and not chew gum?' It is extraordinary how little we know of one another.

There was a first-class negro band, and we never danced to more perfect music. They understand jazz here, and know exactly how to 'put it over'. The American girls are world-famous for their dancing so one cannot go wrong, and as a lot of good dancing men were present also, we had a great time. In deference to training regulations the festivities ended before midnight, but we should all have liked more of it.

August 13

We were off to Forest Hills in good time as the courts were to be closed after one o'clock. There had been a good deal of rain during the night, but the gallery courts, being covered, were fit for play, and we had a couple of hours use of them.

As the tickets for the match were selling well there was every prospect of a good gate, which was cheerful news.

Mrs Chambers received a very charming letter from Mrs Wightman, the donor of the Cup we were playing for, giving us a hearty welcome, and extending to us an invitation from the Longwood Cricket Club to become their guests for the tournament week at Boston; needless to say we were glad to accept.

In the *Evening Sun* appeared an article on the match, and the personnel of the teams, which causes us the most intense amusement. It asserted that 'the British hand and arm' are inferior to the hand and arm of our players, but they can 'match our hand and arm with foot and leg'. Frankly this had us guessing. We did not know whether the American ladies' feet and legs were like hands and arms or what. Miss Colyer was described as a 'stage dancer' and we were told that she is the most frequently photographed player in England, partly because her father is the King's dentist! Miss Fry has the stride of a man, but her father never allowed her to mix her game with short shots! And so on, and so forth. What standard of intelligence can such 'tosh' cater for?

The size of the American newspaper is enormous. An evening paper of thirty sheets is common, most of the morning dailies are of the same weight, whilst the Sunday journals call for the assistance of a black porter to carry them about. They cost three cents, and are by far the cheapest things to be had in the country.

We had a quiet day in view of the big contest on the morrow. One of the most pleasing features of the last few days was the number of messages of hope and encouragement received from friends made in

Canada and elsewhere. Every member of the team was fit and keen and 'on her toes' so we were hopeful of sending them good news.

August 14

The day of the match. All good Americans were 'pulling' for the success of their side as was only natural, and the odds were said to be heavily against us; certainly everything possible was being done to accomplish our downfall. The Clerk of the Weather was early astir and turned on an anti-British day of the most pronounced order! Close, heavy, very humid and terribly hot; he played his part nobly. The patriotic mosquitoes stole upon us during the night, and sought to weaken us by drawing our life's blood from us, and by covering us with minor inflammations. Even the railway porters took a hand in the game of British discomforture.

The first news was that Miss McKane had been stung on the lip by a mosquito causing her entire face to assume enormous proportions. A doctor was hastily summoned, and attended her for two hours. The application of ice bags and other treatment reduced the swelling considerably, but she had more 'lip' all day than is usual with her. Of course Joan Fry would distinguish herself on being asked to help in the treatment! She was requested to apply Ponds Extract – to the wound of course – but thought it would be much more effective to apply Ponds Vanishing Cream to the ice bag! When the latter was applied to the indisposed lip, Miss McKane found her mouth and face deluged with vanishing cream! Everyone was so amused with the story at lunch, that Joan fell off her chair, and almost vanished herself!

Our arrival at Penn Station to catch the train for Forest Hills was rather closely timed (I will not say who was late again) but we could have got it comfortably had not the porter slammed the gate in our faces, as his contribution to our discomforture. This kept us grilling in a stifling atmosphere for half-an-hour awaiting the next train, but we were not dismayed, and persevered against adversity.

The first match was Miss McKane against Mrs Mallory, and was, for us at any rate, of vital importance. A victory would give us a fine start, and strengthen our confidence, and would have an adverse effect on our opponents. Besides we had to wipe out the record of seven matches lost two years ago.

That the interest in the contest is growing by leaps and bounds was proved by excellent attendance of spectators at the start. Their numbers increased to nearly 3000 before the afternoon was over.

The excellent form shown by Miss McKane in recent practices was maintained, notwithstanding the mosquito's attentions, and she took the first set at 6–4. Leading two love in the second, she looked like running away with the match, but Mrs Mallory fought gamely, and forced her into many errors, with the result that the set went to America at 7–5. After an interval of ten minutes which both ladies badly needed, the battle was resumed, but it was soon obvious that Mrs Mallory had shot her bolt in the second set. On the other hand Miss McKane was steady and confident, and went on to win comfortably at 6–0. This gave us the 'one-up' we had set our hearts on, and Miss McKane never rendered a greater service to her country than in winning this match.

My own friendly comments on the game are as follows. Mrs Mallory had all the advantages of ball, climatic conditions, turf and atmosphere but she struck me as being less mobile than she used to be. She still hits the ball hard and early on the top bound, but she is not versatile, and when drawn forward from her beloved baseline, her weaknesses are exposed. Her staying powers under the trying conditions were no greater than her opponent's, and she did not recover as quickly; the spirit was willing, but the flesh could not respond to its demands.

Miss McKane controlled the strange ball very skilfully, and on the whole kept a fine length. Her backhand was working smoothly and well, and she varied her pace and direction cleverly. She did not advance to the net as often as is her wont, but when she did, she seldom, if ever, failed to make the count; for that reason many thought she should have gone up more frequently, but Mrs Mallory's passing shots are very good on both wings, the heat was intense, and I think she was right to nurse her resources, and await her chance of a certain winner. She served rather badly, and would have shortened the match considerably if she had possessed a good drop shot.

In the second contest Miss Fry was up against the American Champion, Miss Helen Wills, and the crowd looked to the latter to retrieve their early misfortune, nor did she fail them. In the first set she played like a champion; her driving on both wings was hard, crisp, and of beautiful length, and she took the first set to love. Miss Fry had not made things difficult for her; she was naturally a little nervous, and being a slow starter, could never get going. But in the second set a complete change came over the scene. The English girl began to time the ball, to hit harder, and find a splendid length. The effect upon Miss Wills was most startling; she lost her pace, and seemed to lose her confidence, and Miss Fry actually took the first four games to love, and at one period scored eleven points in succession. Then Miss Wills played entirely for safety, and was content to hit the ball back, slowly, and with high trajectory, in reliance upon her opponents errors. In this way she crept up to 4–3 but lost the next, and it looked odds on 'set all'. Then things went a little bit wrong for Miss Fry; she missed several golden chances, suffered a bad decision, served a double fault, and lost the set at 7–5.

Playing under the most favourable conditions, and against a young opponent who had had much less experience, Miss Wills' display was disappointing. In the first set her stroke play was beautiful to see, but she is slow of foot, particularly in starting, and is, I think, a slow thinker. In speed and activity she could not compare with Miss Fry, and requires too much time to ever be ranked as Suzanne. Then her complete change of tactics in the second set, was to me a sign of weakness, and not a mere error of judgement. The power and consistency of her ground strokes should enable her to force the pace, and should be used for that purpose, especially when the ball is coming back to her at a good pace, because that is just how she likes it. Yet although Miss Fry was hitting hard, and keeping a good length, Miss Wills assumed a defensive position, and sheathed her deadliest weapon. With weak attacking strokes, defence is often the best, in fact the only means of attack, but with powerful attacking weapons, defence should be forced upon the opposition. Of course if she lost confidence in her driving under Miss Fry's whirlwind attack, that may explain every-thing, but champions do not suffer from that as a rule.

Whatever faults may be found with Miss Fry's style and stroke production, none can question her pluck, her dogged determina-tion, or her speed of foot. It was a great ordeal, and severe test, for a young player of limited first-class experience, knowing her own defects, and the undoubted skill of her opponent, and conscious of the fact that she was playing for her country. To have been overwhelmed in a first set under such circumstances would have shaken the confidence of most, but Miss Fry showed that she is made of the finest metal. The way she went for her great opponent in that second set was a heartening sight; she was here, there and everywhere, and despite a bad attack of 'stitch' never relaxed her efforts. She was beaten, but she gained as much kudos as the winner.

In the third match Mrs Lambert Chambers and Miss Harvey were opposed to Mrs Mallory and Mrs Bundy. There are some who think it was a poor match, but I do not agree with this view. Naturally, it was less exciting than the previous contests, and slower by contrast, because it resolved itself into the 'one-up and one-back' game, which means long rallies between the base liners and an occasional interception, but it was most interesting for more reasons than one. In the first place it is – dare I say it? – twenty years ago since Mrs Chambers and Mrs Bundy were fighting for supremacy at Wimbledon, and to meet again now in International Doubles was a remarkable sight. Then again Mrs Chambers is one of the brainiest players in the world, and on that account is well worth watching, especially by the younger generation. And how she worked in this match! Both Mrs Mallory and her partner seemed determined to keep the ball from Miss Harvey, and to play on to Mrs Chambers for all they were worth, and they did – with consequences not entirely to their satisfaction. Our Captain was as steady as a rock, and gave no change! She hit hard, she hit softly; she forced Mrs Bundy out of court on the side lines, and lobbed and 'dropped' like the artist she is, and kept them thinking and moving all the time. Miss Harvey would chip in now and again with a smash or a volley, but the major portion of the work, and the main credit for the victory, was with Mrs Chambers. The first set was drawn out to 10–8 before it was won, but the second was soon over and we took it at 6–1.

I venture the opinion that the American ladies were not a pair – or rather a team – and that they do not understand the real doubles game, or if they do, they do not play it. Mrs Mallory is not a doubles player, and I believe she dislikes them, and her court-craft and positional play are poor. She made many good shots, and clever placements, but did not combine at all with her partner. Mrs Bundy was very active and occasionally produced something like her one-time famous forehand punch, but she was playing a lone hand all the time, and seemed to have no idea of feeding her partner, whilst her service was extremely poor.

Miss Harvey served well and was particularly safe in her return to service, whilst she also did many good things at the net, but there were occasions when she could have relieved Mrs Chambers of some of the heavy work that was being forced upon her, by a timely interception of Mrs Bundy's lofted returns. No-one feeds her partner more consistently than Mrs Chambers, and the openings she makes ought to produce the maximum number of points.

I only remember one overhead smash in the two singles matches.

At the close of play we were one up – a most happy and gratifying position, and if we felt in particularly good spirits, who will blame us. It left us with two more matches to win in order to retain the Cup, and without being over-confident, we were hopeful.

One must pay tribute to the sporting behaviour of the crowd throughout the matches. Naturally the majority of them wanted the Americans to win, but they were most impartial and generous in their applause and appreciation, and gave our players a great reception. There was one very bad decision on the line against Mrs Chambers and Miss Harvey, and the protests voiced by the crowd had to be silenced by the umpire. This is an example of their fine spirit.

A u g u s t 1 5

Waking early, I saw the sun rise in a glorious sky splashed with tiny rose-coloured clouds, but I could have enjoyed it more had it not been for the thought of those who were to battle in the gathering heat at Forest Hills. There being no comfort in the thought, I banished it, and composed myself to sleep again. The later prospects were no better and it turned out to be a scorcher. Happily the mosquito 'fans' had turned their attention to a visiting baseball team, and had left us alone, and we baulked the railway porters by 'making' the ground in a car.

Women's tennis has never attracted much attention from the populace in America, but the interest aroused by this contest has been unmistakable, and before the first match began there must have been 5000 people within the stadium; later the number in-creased to 6000 which is a record for America as regards a women's match.

Like yesterday, the first round was of vital import to us; a win would make us 3–1, and as we felt confident about the doubles, would give us the victory, but a loss would make it possible for the Americans to recover the Cup, regardless of the doubles. Happily for us our fate was in the hands of the Captain, who was not likely to be disturbed by the importance of the occasion. Miss Goss had won the right to contest this single by her victory over Miss Brown, the American Captain, in the trials, and in addition to a fine service, has a strong back-hand drive. The first set was very evenly fought and went to 7–5 before Mrs Chambers annexed it; most people thought that the long tussle in the heat rendered it imperative that Mrs Chambers should win in straight sets, as if it went to a third set the better staying powers of the younger player must give her the match. As Miss Goss won the second at 6–3 it remained to be seen whether this assumption was correct. The ten minutes interval allowed was of great service to both players, but Mrs Chambers utterly confounded the 'knowalls' by playing her opponent to a standstill. She fed her strong back-hand until she got her out of position and then hit her fast cross-drive to the forehand, with fatal results to Miss Goss, or drew her forward with a beautiful drop shot and passed her across the court or with a deep well-timed lob. It was the brainiest display of lawn tennis one could wish to see, and Miss Goss was powerless against it. Taking the set 6–1 and the match, Mrs Chambers left the court amidst a tumult of applause from friend and foe alike. Everyone present, knowing anything about the game, recognised that they had witnessed a marvellous performance, and could not refrain from paying tribute to the master mind. Personally I would not have missed this match for anything as it is doubtful if one will ever have the opportunity of seeing such another.

The excitement that had temporarily subsided arose again when Miss Helen Wills and Miss McKane entered the court.

For America, it was now or never and local hopes and confidence were centred in the young champion. She began in irresistible style, her ground strokes on both wings being crisp and beautifully placed; she also served well mixing her deliveries cleverly, and Miss McKane was never able to settle down to her best game. The loss of the first set at 1–6 only brought out her well-known fighting qualities however, and there was quite a different story to tell in the second. She got her service working more effectively, and used fine judgement in going up to the net, blocking many of Miss Wills' hot returns, and aceing everything possible. This treatment seemed to unsettle the latter and again she resorted to the incomprehensible methods used against Miss Fry the day before. Every return was tossed high in the air, deep enough to make smashing risky, but whether she did it to obtain a rest, or to tempt Miss McKane to smash, I cannot say; however, it did not pay as she lost the set 1–6 and we were all square. The third set was a magnificent struggle; Miss Wills went to 5–2 and looked to have the match in her pocket, but the English lady then made a magnificent recovery, and took three games in succession. It was 5 all, 6 all and 7 all, and Miss McKane missed a 'sitter' for the vantage game owing to losing sight of the ball against the background of white attire on the stand. That was bad luck, but the Fates did not forgive, and Miss Wills took the set at 9–7, and the match.

During the last set, the excitement of sections of the crowd, burst its bounds, and there were some unpleasant demonstrations against the umpire and linesmen. It was unfortunate that one linesman should have yielded to the pressure of outside opinion to the extent of reversing his decision, thereby compelling the umpire to do the same, as it only encouraged further excesses on the part of the crowd. Of course most of the decisions criticised by the spectators were perfectly correct, and where errors were made, they had no effect on the result.

With a chance of still pulling the match out of the fire Mrs Mallory displayed her very best form against Miss Fry. It was a baseline contest, pure and simple, with both players hitting hard and keep-ing a fine length, but Mrs Mallory was the more consistent, and won on her opponent's errors. She took the first at 6–3 and the next at 6–0 but notwithstanding the score, Miss Fry played better in the second than in the first. Some of the rallies were truly remarkable; on one occasion the ball passed over the net thirty times at least, and when Miss Fry finished it with a cross volley, the spectators rose en masse, and applauded for quite two minutes. They had not settled down however, and some of the remarks shouted out during this match were in shocking taste to say the least of it.

Three all with the doubles to play as the decider. That was the position, and although it was getting towards six-thirty few people left the stadium. Miss McKane and Miss Wills had been receiving the attentions of the masseuse, and needed all the rest they could get, and in the meantime, Miss Brown and Miss Colyer came on to court and indulged in a prolonged knock-up. Then Miss McKane made her appearance and had a fine reception, but there was no Miss Wills. Time crept on, and the crowd lost their heads and behaved disgracefully. Twenty-five minutes elapsed before Miss Wills made her appearance, and she was then received with a mingled outburst of applause, hissing and booing, without knowing the cause of it. It appears that Miss Wills had conceded to Miss McKane the first use of the masseuse, and had then to take her turn; the Mallory-Fry match was over much sooner than had been expected, and so the trouble arose. I think it would have been better if none of the players had been allowed to enter the arena until Miss Wills was ready, as that would at least have prevented a demonstration against her alone.

The final and deciding match was over in 25 minutes. The English pair took the first nine games straight off the reel, were checked for a few minutes in the second set, and then went out – 6–0, 6–3. It was one of the most brilliant exhibitions of the doubles game one could wish to see, and if Miss Colyer was more prominent than her partner, it was because Miss McKane played so beautifully as to give her the opportunities she revelled in. Their team work was excellent, and in this respect they were far ahead of the American pair, who were merely two persons playing together without combination of any kind. It was a sparkling finish, and although the crowd continued to be noisy, they gave the winners a great reception at the end.

The Cup, filled with crimson roses, was presented to Mrs Lambert Chambers on the court, amid the hearty and sincere congratulations of the American team and the many officials present. It was a great day for the old country, and everyone seemed to be genuinely delighted that she had staged such a brilliant and successful 'comeback'. One wag in the crowd raised a shout of laughter, when he asked in a loud voice 'why England didn't play the women in her Davis Cup Team'.

Despite the conduct of the spectators – or rather, of a few of them – the match can have left nothing but the happiest memories in the minds of those concerned in it. Friendliness, fine sportsmanship, and courtesy marked the proceedings from beginning to end.

There are comparatively few people at home who will be able to appreciate the true value of the achievement of our team. They had to contend with the pick of the women players of America playing in their own setting, and in a wholly sympathetic atmosphere; they had less than two weeks to accustom themselves to a damp and enervating but intense heat, the like of which we seldom, if ever, experience at home; and they had to adapt themselves to a ball that is lighter, comes off the ground quicker, and bounds higher than the one they know. To overcome all these difficulties they needed not merely skill, adaptability and patience, but the finest grit and determination, and their success proved that they possessed all of these.

Mrs Lambert Chambers may well be proud of the team she led so tactfully and so brilliantly.

Mrs Chambers had certainly led her team intelligently, a point well stressed on the return home of this team with the Cup: Mrs Dorothea Chambers, Kitty, Evelyn Colyer, Joan Fry and Ermyntrude Harvey.

To this Wightman Cup triumph was added the fine efforts of Kitty in the American championships that followed. She not only won the mixed doubles with the Australian Jack Hawkes – having beaten Tilden and Mrs Mallory in the semi final – but also reached the final of the singles. There she lost to Helen Wills 6–3, 0–6, 2–6, but had beaten Elizabeth Ryan in the quarter finals, and Mrs Mallory in the semi final. The latter was considered her win of the year as she recovered from 5–3 down in the final set to win 4–6, 7–5, 8–6.

But in reality her 'win of the year' lay just ahead – her marriage to Leslie Godfree.

In Wightman Cup tennis there was to be one further critical moment on the centre court. In 1930 she and Phoebe Holcroft-Watson faced the two Helens – Wills-Moody and Jacobs – in the decisive rubber of that year's Wightman Cup. Amidst tense excitement they won back the trophy last held in 1925 with a last ditch 7–5, 1–6, 6–4 victory.

8

The World Championships

It was remarkable how quickly Kitty caught the eye of the English selectors. A new girl to the school of tennis in 1919, that very same summer she was chosen to play in the World covered courts championships held at the Sporting Club de Paris where she won the doubles with Mrs Beamish as a consolation for being beaten in the semi final of the singles. That was a good enough start for the new girl.

But four years later, in 1923, she went even better when the same competition was organised in Barcelona. There she won all three titles, beating Mrs Beamish in the singles final 6–3, 4–6, 6–2; the doubles, with Mrs Beamish as her partner, and the mixed with W C Crawley.

Here she won a handsome gold cup presented by the Queen of Spain, a prize she treasured so much that in later life she had to stop polishing it. Yet she felt embarrassed by that victory. Having arrived at the stadium for the match she discovered she had left all her rackets behind at the hotel. And since they were due on court in a few minutes, with no time to chase back to the hotel, Mrs Beamish lent her second racket to Kitty who proceeded to beat her sporting adversary.

Having shaken the dust of Barcelona off her feet Kitty took a playing trip to the South of France – to Cannes, Monte Carlo, Mentone, and Nice. This was Suzanne Lenglen's stamping ground, but Kitty met her only once in the final at Mentone where the French mega-star won 6–2, 7–5. But there was one feather in her cap. In the semi final she had beaten her *bête noire*, Elizabeth Ryan, 7–5, 2–6, 6–2. Yet generally that trip to the Cote d'Azur reaped little reward beyond the glorious Mediterranean weather, the charms of the setting and the beautiful flowers. It was naturally, a relaxing change from English weather.

In those days there was yet another important, pompous sounding competition, the world hard court championships – long since forgotten. The first of these took place in Brussels in 1922. Discovering that Suzanne Lenglen had entered, Kitty made tracks for the Belgian capital determined to try to get a set off the champion.

She almost did. It was in the semi final that the pair met. Kitty led 5–4 in the opening set and had a set point. Having missed it she then led 6–5 and 8–7. But overplaying her net attack she lost the set at 8–10. In the second set she led again at 2–1 but Lenglen turned the screw a little and won the last five games for victory. Kitty learned a lesson that day against Lenglen – not to overdo a net attack without a good opening ground stroke.

The next year this championship was staged at St Cloud, an outer suburb of Paris. Again Kitty found herself face to face with Lenglen. This time it was the final but Kitty, caught perhaps between two stools, baseline and net play, was full of unforced errors from which Suzanne benefitted to win 6–3, 6–3.

But something good was in store for Kitty. Partnering Mrs Beamish in the doubles they beat Lenglen and Mme Golding in the final 6–3, 6–2. This was the second time Kitty had left a court having got the better of Lenglen in doubles. She now believes she is the only British girl to have achieved that twice.

In 1920, just a year after joining the tennis circuit, Kitty found herself picked for the Olympic Games. These were held at Antwerp in Belgium. Kitty got to the semi final but withdrew to sustain her energies for the doubles events. However she beat a Mme Fick in the third place play-off which gained her a bronze medal.

But more was to come. She won the doubles with Mrs McNair thereby collecting a gold medal, a prize worth every ounce since the two of them inflicted a first doubles defeat on Lenglen. A silver medal then followed in the mixed when she reached the final with Max Woosman, who also played football as an amateur for Manchester City. A gold, a silver and a bronze was a good haul for one so young and in her first Olympic games.

The next Olympics, held in Paris in 1924, proved to be the last for tennis, the reason for which will be explained at the end of this chapter by Mr Basil Hutchins, a member of the All England Club, who actually accompanied Kitty to Los Angeles for the Olympics of 1984 as representatives of the Wimbledon championships.

In Paris, those sixty odd years ago, Kitty again returned home with two medals – a silver and a bronze. The silver for a doubles final with Mrs Covell, and a bronze for winning a third place play-off in the singles. The reigning champion for all those years is none other than Mrs Helen Wills-Roark, (formerly Wills-Moody) of America, until some-one succeeds her at the next medal winning ceremony at Seoul in 1988.

The pattern of events, separating the disappearance and reappear-ance of tennis as an Olympic sport, is recorded by Hutchins:

On August 14, 1983 Mrs Kathleen Godfree received a letter from the Southern California Committee for the Olympic Games asking if she, along with all other 1924 medallists, would like to attend the 1984 Summer Olympic Games in Los Angeles given that the number of people involved would be acceptable. Mrs Godfree was one of the first to reply in the affirmative. In January 1984 she received another letter in which the President of the Southern California Committee for the Olympic Games conveyed his sincere apologies for having to rescind the previous invitation to attend the Games as the number of those 1924 medallists who had intimated their wish to travel to Los Angeles was in excess of 60, and as such would present too many difficulties. Realising that this news must have been a matter of deep disappointment to Mrs Godfree some senior members of The All England Lawn Tennis and Croquet Club, among them Russell Young, Neville Hooper and John Archer approached the Chairman of the Club, Buzzer Hadingham, with the suggestion that perhaps there existed the possibility of inviting her to go to the Olympics as a representative of the Wimbledon championships. This suggestion was seized upon by the Chairman and, with the full support of Jim Cochrane, the President of the Lawn Tennis Association, the invita-tion was reinstated and readily accepted by Mrs Godfree.

I was delighted to be asked by the Chairman to escort Mrs Godfree on the trip, and I am aware that the invitation was prompted by the fact that as a member of the British Olympic Association and the British Film Institute opportunities would exist to plan a varied programme covering a wide spectrum of events.

In January 1984 Dr Cyril M White, Professor of Sociology at the National University of Ireland in Dublin, working on plans to celebrate the 75th anniversary of the University, discovered that one of the founders, John Peers Boland, Member of Parliament in

London from 1900 – 1918 was the first Olympic Tennis Champion in Athens in 1896. He won the singles and also the doubles with Fritz Travers of Austria. The first matches were played in a tent and others outside in the centre of the velodrome. The winners received diplomas.

Boland was the scholar-athlete type idealised by Baron Pierre de Coubertin, founder of the modern Olympics. Tennis continued to be part of the Olympics until 1924, but not without some problems. At the 1912 event in Stockholm for example the dates conflicted with Wimbledon, precluding British and United States players participating, although one US player competed on his own. Before the 1920 Games in Antwerp the Belgian authorities received a request from the USLTA to change the dates to July, but as they were unable to do so the US team withdrew. Thirteen nations did send teams and Suzanne Lenglen won the ladies singles and mixed doubles with Mrs McNair.

The year 1924 turned out to be not only the biggest but the best Olympic Tennis Tournament, but also the last. Twenty-eight countries sent a total of 113 players, 82 men and 31 women, to Paris. The US won all five events. Ironically, just when the Olympic Tennis competition was reaching its zenith the party came to an end. Over a period of years friction developed between the International Lawn Tennis Federation and the International Olympic Committee. The ILTF wanted to control the rules and officials for the Olympic Tennis event and also requested a seat on the IOC. The IOC meanwhile jealously guarded its right to appoint its own members and turned down the ILTF request. Adding insult to injury the IOC suggested that perhaps the ILTF could suspend the All-England championships at Wimbledon during Olympic years. Needless to say the ILTF and Wimbledon officials issued a firm 'no'. The two sides reached an impasse, the ILTF withdrew from the Games and tennis disappeared from the Olympics not to resurface until 44 years later when it was added as an exhibition, non-medal, sport in 1968 at the Games in Mexico. Since 1968 when Spain's Manuel Santana defeated countryman Manuel Orantes in the men's singles and Helga Niessen of West Germany beat Peaches Bartkowicz of the USA in the womens' final, the ILTF (now the ITF) and the USLTA (now the USTA) made repeated attempts to have tennis reinstated as an Olympic sport.

The movement gained much needed momentum when Phillipe Chatrier, a long time supporter of Olympic tennis, was elected President of the ITF and the breakthrough came in 1978 when Chatrier convinced Jack Kramer, founder of the powerful men's Grand Prix professional circuit, that tennis in the Olympics would help tennis flourish around the world. As an extra incentive the prospect of holding a tennis event in Los Angeles in 1984 would help raise funds for a brand new tennis stadium in the area; this could be used at a later date for other major tennis events in California. In March 1980 the IOC approved the inclusion of tennis as a demonstration sport along with baseball for the 1984 Olympics. Shortly after, agreement was reached in principle that this facility should be extended to a full medal-winning sport in Seoul in 1988.

But that was just the beginning. In March 1983 the IOC decreed that the demonstration sport of tennis would be open to any person, twenty years or under, in good standing with the ITF. In other words the Olympic tennis event was going to welcome, for the first time, recognised professional athletes. This in itself represents enormous problems for the IOC when it comes to the rules and guidelines for the 1988 Games in Seoul. In spite of this the 1984 tennis event was highly successful. Some 6000 seats per day, in the attractive new stadium at UCLA, were sold out weeks before. Indeed, of all the events which took place in Los Angeles, tickets for tennis were more difficult to obtain than most. Even with an under-twenties tournament of the attraction of Cash, Arias, Edberg, Reggi, Graf, Horvath and Jaeger was enough to excite the public. In 1988 it could be that Becker and Navratilova will compete for the honour of winning a gold medal. Given that the event only demands one week of the top players' time every four years, why not? Today the facts are that top athletes in track and field are currently earning very large sums of money. The system under which athletes are remunerated goes back to the IAAF meeting in Athens in 1982 when it was argued that trust funds could be set up into which appearance money would go. From these trust funds athletes would be allowed to draw money for things like travel, hotel and general expenses. All remaining monies would then be frozen until the day when the athletes retired. Like most professional sports the leading athletes can command huge sums; for example, Carl Lewis has been offered $100,000 for one meeting, and Ed Moses regularly picks up around $35,000 for each appearance. Others like Coe and Cram can also demand substantial sums. In addition these athletes can earn large fees from advertising companies and from the media.

However, the drawback with paying appearance money is the same as the world of tennis experienced in the fifties and sixties, mainly that appearance in itself does not guarantee good spectator sport, and the competitors are not obliged to give maximum effort within their own event.

The IAAF retaliated with a new formula for paying athletes in 1985 when they initiated a Grand Prix circuit similar in many ways with the tennis Grand Prix. There would be fifteen meetings and one final and the participation of individual athletes would be as a result of negotiation. Points would be awarded for placings in each event, nine for first, seven for second, six for third and so on. Those athletes with the most points from their five best meetings would be invited to a Grand Prix final in Rome where they were to receive prize money to the tune of £7,900 for each winner, £5,500 for second and so on until the eighth place which carries a prize of £790. The IAAF are to be congratulated for their attempt to 'clean up' the sport as happened in tennis in 1968. No money was paid to any athlete for participation in the Olympic Games, but obviously, as in tennis, the medallists would gain enormously once the Games were over.

As British representatives of Wimbledon, Kitty and Hutchins were wined and dined and attended receptions on every day of their eleven day visit. She was presented to Princess Anne and to Prince Philip, who were there for the show jumping events, and to many of the British competitors. Kitty contacted Helen Wills-Roark, as holder of the Olympic title all those years ago, but could not persuade her to attend the Games. In the event she handed over the Waterford crystal vase to the United States Lawn Tennis Association President to be passed on to Helen who had failed to attend the Wimbledon parade of lady champions in 1984.

While in Los Angeles Kitty had also run into A E Porritt, of New Zealand, another competitor in Paris in 1924, who had run to a bronze medal against Harold Abrahams. Kitty and Porritt had not seen each other for sixty years. 'I'm eighty-four now', said Porritt proudly. 'I'm eighty-eight' replied Kitty quietly.

When they returned home from the 1984 Olympics Hutchins wrote this: 'I must record my total admiration for the way in which Kitty entered into the spirit of every detail of the tour. I realised that the programme itself might prove to be pretty demanding, especially in such a hot climate, but her response was so very exceptional that everyone was thrilled to meet her and be in her company. At her age she was indeed an incredible lady and an example to us all.'

That meeting with A E Porritt, at the Los Angeles Olympics, stirred Kitty's memories of her own involvement in 1920 and 1924 at Amsterdam and Paris. Tennis then was only a supporting item in the programme and not as universally popular as today. But Kitty remembered the part they all played in the opening ceremony – the march of the various national teams into the stadium proceded by a flagbearer. The British team, on each occasion, she thinks, was comprised of four men and four women, chosen by the Lawn Tennis Association.

The medal ceremonies, too, were much the same as they are today. There were steps up to the rostrum for the gold, silver and bronze medals, the winner's national flag fluttering in the breeze and the national anthems to stir the blood and the feeling of loyalty. All this Kitty could sense again, remembering the gold, two silver and two bronze medals she herself had collected all those years ago with Mrs McNair, Mrs Covell and Max Woosnam. Woosnam's medal, in fact, is now in the Wimbledon museum.

But a cloud now hangs over the Seoul Olympics of 1988. With politics invading sport more and more and a number of problems upsetting both race and religious relations amongst nations, a short fuse is burning under certain sporting events. The South African connection is the cause of much unpheaval which has recently disrupted cricket, rugby football and athletics.

With those points in mind David Miller, for one, has waved a warning flag in *The Times*:

TENNIS LINKS WITH S AFRICA COULD THREATEN GAMES

The Olympic Games are about to discover that with tennis they have invited an embarrassing house guest to Seoul. It is evident from Eastern European and Third World representatives attending the first international congress of Sport For All, that there will be a protest and potential boycott against players on the anti-apartheid banned list. That list includes Boris Becker, the Wimbledon champion, who played in South Africa as a junior.

Also on the banned list are such players as Arias, Bale, Buhning, Connors, Gerulaitis, Glickstein, Gunthardt, Mayotte, McNamee, Teltscher and Vilas. There can be no doubt that tennis poses a far more serious threat to the stability of the Games than rugby, a non-Olympic sport. This is an issue which the International Olympic Committee and International Tennis Federation must quickly resolve. South Africa makes Soviet blood boil even faster than professionalism does.

9

O v e r s e a s   T o u r s

Sportsmen and women and members of the sporting media are often able to see more of the world than members of many other professions. If they are intelligent they widen their horizons and add to their knowledge of places and people. They can count themselves lucky.

With the worldwide spread of sport the modern games player is a member of the jet set, leaping from continent to continent, earning vast sums of money if successful, and living a life wrapped in cotton wool luxury.

This was not quite the same for the amateur players of the 1920s. Nonetheless Kitty for one, within a decade, visited nine or ten countries. Three times she went to America, and twice to Canada for a month each time. She spent four months in South Africa (October 1925 to February 1926) and visited France, Germany, Belgium, Holland, Scandinavia, Czechoslovakia, Spain and Southern Ireland. These visits have left memories of one sort or another that survive to this day.

The South African tour was particularly testing physically. The party of four women and four men comprised Kitty, Mrs Watson, Miss Colyer, Miss Ridley, L A Godfree (Captain), G R Crole Rees (Manager), C G Eames and M V Summerson.

They travelled thousands of miles by train and car (often on rough dusty roads) to play twenty matches, of which they won sixteen, drew one, and lost three. The itinerary included three test matches, of which one was won, one drawn and one lost.

Matches were played at differing altitudes and often in great heat. This affected some of the team, especially Kitty, who found the conditions particularly trying. It was decided not to play her in singles for the third test but to keep her to doubles which she bravely did while not fully fit.

The South African hospitality was very generous wherever they travelled; they were taken to diamond and gold mines, and visited many of the historic areas of the Boer War, in particular Ladysmith.

However, for all the testing moments one happy event came about – the marriage of Leslie Godfree and Kitty on January 18, 1926. They separated from the rest of the team at Kimberley to stay with friends Mr and Mrs Lezard. It was in their house that a judge performed the simple ceremony which Leslie and Kitty kept from the rest of their party. When Leslie finally revealed the event on board ship to the press and their own colleagues just before departing for home, there was considerable surprise and not a little hurt for not being let into the secret earlier. The reason why they were kept in the dark was that the happy couple wished to write to their parents in England before the news hit the newpaper headlines – which they certainly did in England. Interestingly there was no telephone, radio or telegraph, at that time, capable of reaching England that was available to anyone other than the press.

Five years after the South African trip, however, there came a period of worry. In 1931, on a tour of Scandinavia with F J Perry as her doubles partner in a team of men and women, Kitty was in Oslo when a telephone message came from her sister Margaret and from Fred Perry's father to say that Leslie had been injured in a car accident. Apparently he was being driven by a friend to play a match at Cambridge against the University when there was a crash with another car at a crossroads near St Albans. Leslie, lucky to be alive, in a car which somersaulted twice, suffered several broken ribs and a punctured lung. He was in hospital. Fortunately Kitty was at the end of her tour of Scandinavia.

Leslie actually had to stay in hospital for several months but was fully recovered on his return home, never to be worried by his injuries in later life. This was a great relief to Kitty who, by then, had a two year old son, David, to look after.

It can be recorded that neither of the drivers ever made contact with Leslie again, not even to enquire after his health.

As for the tour itself, these were the manager's reactions:

Of the ladies, Miss McKane, Mrs Watson and Miss Colyer all played consistently well, particularly Mrs Watson who at times played better than she has ever done at home, and I think as a result of this tour she has definitely improved her game. I strongly recommend that Mrs Watson be awarded her colours, as she is thoroughly deserving of them. Miss Ridley was disappointing, more particularly in Ladies Doubles, as in most games it was Mrs Watson who bore the entire brunt of the matches. I do not think Miss Ridley's tennis has improved as a result of the tour.

If the International Match Committee are intending nominating pairs for Wimbledon this year, I would suggest that Miss McKane (now Mrs Godfree) and Miss Colyer should be nominated as a pair. I am quite convinced they form a very strong combination.

Of the men, both Crole Rees and Summerson were most dis-appointing. The latter commenced very well and struck form as quickly as anyone in the team, but after a short time appeared to be thoroughly upset by the conditions of play, and undoubtedly lost his confidence and latterly played very poorly. It is only fair to him however to say that he was undoubtedly very considerably affected by the intense heat. Crole Rees practically never struck form during the tour, and from his own account appears to have been worried by his duties as Manager, but in all fairness I do not think too much stress should be laid on this point, as in many instances it was his temperament and entire lack of confidence that caused his undoing. His record in singles was really poor as he was defeated on many occasions by opponents very much weaker than himself, and often in some matches he only obtained one or two games. Eames was consistently good and always played with a very stout heart.

Suggestions for consideration in connection with another team's visit to South Africa:

1   There is no doubt that the greatest problem is the amount of travelling in connection with the tour, and it is suggested that a team might travel via the Mediterranean and down the East Coast of Africa to Beira and commence the land travelling from there. If this could be done, it would save at least 50% of actual travelling in South Africa, although it is understood it would lengthen the tour by two to three weeks. This suggestion might have the additional advantage of enabling those responsible for

working out the itinerary to avoid the rather sudden changes from low to high altitude, as there is no doubt these sudden changes from low to high altitude and vice versa do have a very marked effect both on the health of the team and the actual game itself.

2   Time should be allowed for any further team visiting Johannesburg to have at least four or five days there before being called upon to play a match, so as to have a good opportunity of becoming acclimatised. The present team arrived in Johannesburg on a Thursday afternoon and played its first match on the following Saturday, a matter of roughly forty hours.

3   In a hot climate of this nature a ten minutes rest should be provided for in the event of set-all being reached. The arrangement during the present tour not to play more than three sets was undoubtedly very necessary, otherwise the strain would be too great on the players.

4   One of the chief difficulties experienced by the team was the absence, almost without exception, of any screens or other suitable background at the ends of the court. One realises in the present tour, how difficult it would have been to provide any such background as under existing conditions, in most of the centres played in, it would have meant depriving a very large number of spectators of a proper view of the matches. There is no doubt however it is a very serious handicap, and one which should as far as possible be remedied. The only centre where a really excellent background was provided was at Bloemfontein, and as a result the team played some of its best tennis there.

5   It would be of immense assistance if a baggage man or boy could be provided for the team. With a team of 8 people there is bound to be a large amount of luggage, and its constant removal from the train to hotels and vice versa causes a large amount of unnecessary trouble to the Manager, which could be avoided by the above suggestion. It seems perhaps a small matter, but from practical experience it is a suggestion which if acted upon would prove of the greatest possible assistance.

6   The question of a more suitable time of the year for a tour should be taken into consideration. One was being constantly told the team had come out at the wrong time, and possibly it would be better to leave England earlier in the year.

7   In many centres two courts were often used at the same time. I would suggest this should be avoided as far as possible, as it is very disconcerting and the applause accorded to one match, often at a critical phase of the other match, tends largely to increase the difficulties of the players.

General Remarks

I cannot close this report without putting on record my sincere appreciation of all that has been done for the team, not only by the officials of the South African Lawn Tennis Union, but by the officials of all the various Provinces and centres the team has visited. Everywhere we have been treated with great consideration and courtesy and the greatest possible sportsmanship has been extended to us. It is invidious perhaps to mention names but one cannot help referring to Mr H J Lamb, the President of the South African Lawn Tennis Union and 'Father' of lawn tennis in South Africa. He has spared himself nothing; meeting us on arrival at Cape Town and travelling with us for a fortnight; his help and advice which were ever at my disposal were absolutely invaluable. After Mr Lamb left the team, Mr P D Jackson travelled with us to Johannesburg, and on our visit to Rhodesia we were accompanied by Mr Du Toit and to both these gentlemen I extend warmest thanks for their kindness and consideration. This principle of sending a responsible official of the South African Lawn Tennis Union is one to be heartily approved, as it is of immense help, and assistance, to the Captain of a visiting team.

On our journeys through South Africa, a special coach was placed at our disposal by the South African Railways, largely through the influence of Mr Thompson, and one cannot adequately express how much this kindly consideration materially added to the comfort of the team during its long and often tiring journeys. Our grateful thanks to the authorities and those concerned in arranging the concession.

One cannot but refer to the truly wonderful reception the team received everywhere it went, the spectators were most sporting and enthusiastic and thoroughly appreciated every point of the play.

In conclusion the following extract from a letter I received from Mr H J Lamb may be of interest: 'I think that sufficient has been said at tennis gatherings which you have attended and by the press of this country to convince you that from our point of view the tour has been a great success' . . . 'Nothing will give me greater pleasure than to convey to the Lawn Tennis Association our deep appreciation of their action in sending us the team and of the services they have rendered South African lawn tennis.'

Once again I have to thank the Committee for the great honour accorded me in being asked to captain the team, an honour which I much appreciate.

If there is any further information that may be required I shall be only too pleased to do what I can.

The results of the tour were as follows:

Singles

	Played	Won	Lost	Unfinished
Miss McKane	7	7	0	0
Mrs Watson	14	11	3	0
Miss Ridley	6	4	2	0
Miss Colyer	1	1	0	0
Crole Rees	12	2	10	0
Summerson	14	5	9	0
Eames	1	1	0	0

Ladies Doubles

	Played	Won	Lost	Unfinished
Miss McKane & Miss Colyer	13	13	0	0
Miss McKane & Mrs Watson	1	1	0	0
Mrs Watson & Miss Ridley	11	9	2	0
Mrs Watson & Miss Colyer	3	3	0	0
Miss Colyer & Miss Ridley	2	2	0	0

Gent's Doubles

	Played	Won	Lost	Unfinished
Godfree & Eames	15	11	4	0
Crole Rees & Summerson	15	9	4	2
Godfree & Summerson	3	1	2	0
Eames & Crole Rees	2	1	1	0

Mixed Doubles

	Played	Won	Lost	Unfinished
Godfree & Miss McKane	15	12	1	2
Eames & Miss Colyer	15	12	3	0
Crole Rees & Mrs Watson	3	3	0	0
Summerson & Miss Ridley	4	3	1	0
Godfree & Miss Colyer	2	2	0	0
Eames & Mrs Watson	1	1	0	0
Crole Rees & Miss Ridley	1	1	0	0

Looking back now to her American and Canadian trips Kitty remembers New York as a hectic city where everything and everybody moved at great speed and where she felt it was difficult to breathe in hot weather because of the skyscrapers. 'I enjoyed it very much; so much to do, so many theatres, so much to see. But I couldn't live there. But there were some lovely country clubs where we practised and received such friendly entertainment.'

Quebec in Canada particularly interested her. The city, being half-French, intrigued her and she was impressed with the history of General Wolfe storming the heights of Quebec. 'The St Lawrence River was very impressive and when we finally sailed for home the sunsets were quite glorious.'

In 1927 there was a trip to Prague when England played Czechoslovakia. After the match a Czech Count, owner of a large vineyard, invited the three English women players out to dinner at his estate, twenty miles outside the city. They were given a lift in his fast Hispano-Suiza car. He drove at a speed around 100 mph, but since it was an open car the three girls in the back seat became cold and dishevelled.

One of the girls asked Kitty if she could ask the Count to drive more slowly. So Kitty moved forward and tapped the man on his shoulder. The Count turned back quickly to enquire the reason and in the act of turning found his toupé blown off by the rush of wind. He rescued it with a grab and apologised with some embarrassment. In those days to lose a toupé was as awkward as losing false teeth.

Repairs done and speed reduced a delightful evening was had at the Count's fine chateau. Dinner was enjoyed by candlelight, the table covered with bottles of wine. Before the drive back to the city Kitty and the others once again asked the Count to drive more slowly. He apologised once more, saying: 'I'm so sorry. I'd forgotten how slowly you English drive.'

In those days when many players went to Dublin after Wimbledon, Kitty went there with a purpose in 1924. She had an Irish boyfriend who was in the jewellery business and she had accumulated some £80 worth of vouchers on Mappin & Webb from 'winnings' of domestic tournaments. But she didn't want a diamond ring or piece of jewellery, she wanted a car.

So the boyfriend hatched a plot. He and Kitty went to Mappin & Webb and selected and bought a diamond ring. Then they travelled to

Ireland where the boyfriend sold the ring handsomely, being in the business, and then off they went to visit a friend of his who owned a garage.

Kitty liked the look of a pretty little green two-seater open car and, with the money raised from the sale of the ring, she bought her first motor car. She was thrilled.

She played at the Fitzwilliam Club but was so excited with her new acquisition that she can't remember anything about the tournament, except that she could now drive from where she was staying to the tennis club in comfort for the first time.

The tournament over, and research reveals she won all three titles, she had to return to London and home. So in her little green open tourer she drove from Dublin to Dun Laoghaire, caught the night ferry to Holyhead on Anglesey in North Wales and from there drove to London without mishap. How delighted she was. The car behaved perfectly and was a 'great prize' for getting her round to the various tournaments.

However, she was very concerned for years as to what the very strict Lawn Tennis Association of those days might do if they found out what she had done. Would they consider this an act of professionalism? They never found out as she told no one. In fact it was only about three or four years ago that she actually let on to her family and then, in one of her many interviews, she told the story – some sixty years after the event. She doesn't think there will be any repercussions now!

10

Footprints of the Years

Having been involved in the All-England championships for sixty-eight years, sixteen of them as a competitor, one is entitled to become a little weighed down by memories of events and players. This has been Kitty's burden; she has seen so much.

In attempting to set down her more exciting and important memories it has to be remembered that tennis is a divided game. It has a singles and a doubles. The truth is that players, on the whole, are judged by their quality as a singles player, but there is so much to enjoy and admire in good doubles play.

In certain ways they are different games, perhaps comparable with individual figure skating, and pairs skating or dancing. Certainly the tactics are very different. I pressed Kitty on this subject and she decided to deal with some men and women she had not mentioned earlier in our discussions, and to follow this appraisal with a few doubles pairs that had caught her attention.

She had seen Bill Tilden win the singles titles of 1920 and 1921, both at the old Worple Road ground, but had missed his 1930 victory at Wimbledon because of the birth of her first son. From what she saw of him then, and thinking about him now, she feels that with modern rackets and balls, and with sterner fitness training, he would probably become the world's number one as he was in his day.

Apparently he had five different types of service, and had not only a variety of strokes but also held a masterly knowledge of the game in all its phases. If he had a weakness it was his temperament which occasionally, for no explained reason, could let him down. An example of this proved to be one of the sensations of Wimbledon during the reign of the 'four musketeers'.

He was playing Cochet on the centre court and led the Frenchman by two sets to love, 5–1 and 40–15. He was at match point and virtually home and dry when the unbelievable came to pass. He lost the point, the game and eventually the match. It was not that he tired; simply and suddenly he lost control. Unfortunately, it appears that his lack of physical and mental strengths in his other walks of life finally led to his death in 1953 aged 63, a mental, moral and physical wreck. A wonderful player with a sad ending.

Next to Tilden, Kitty used to enjoy watching Fred Perry. In fact he was her partner in mixed doubles on a Scandinavian tour in 1931 before he had won the first of his three consecutive singles titles. Already world champion at table tennis he was obviously heading for the big time. Extremely fit and trained to a 'T' by Arsenal footballers at Highbury, he told Kitty he never minded a five set match. He felt he could always outlast and wear down his opponent.

Next she was struck by Rod Laver, the Australian 'rocket', a brilliant left hander with devastating top spin drives on both wings and a deadly volleyer. He achieved the grand slam twice in 1962 and 1969. The only other man to have pulled off the grand slam was Donald Budge, the American, who was noted for his backhand which he seemed to play in an unorthodox style with the back of his hand facing the net. Fast, with great control, in 1937 and 1938 he won the singles, doubles and mixed doubles, which has only been equalled by Bobby Riggs, of America, in 1939 and by Frank Sedgman, the Australian, in 1952.

Thirty years ago one of the finest of the rising young Australian champions was Lew Hoad. He had wrists of steel. He was able to play almost every type of shot. Kitty was first impressed by his doubles play, in partnership with Ken Rosewall. The Australian Lawn Tennis Association sent Hoad and Rosewall over when they were both still teenagers and they quickly made a mark, winning the doubles in 1953 and 1956. Lew Hoad also won the singles in 1956 and 1957, beating Rosewall in the first of those finals. Ken, beaten in four finals was one of the best men never to have lifted the title. Beautifully stylish, with a classic backhand, his service was his weak spot. His foure finals were stretched across twenty years, an extraordinary length of time.

Of recent stars Borg, McEnroe, Connors and Lendl, have been top of Kitty's modern list. Of these Borg, winner of five titles in succession, was a fine example in behaviour. A double handed backhand with a whipped top spin, he seemed to have ice in his veins. He was a fine match player who never questioned a line call and who possessed a cold concentration like a superb poker player. McEnroe, a New Yorker, was, and is, a natural, instinctive player with a great range of shots and volleys. Sadly he ruins his play on occasions by his explosive character which has dragged tennis into the gutter.

Connors, another American, is a tremendous fighter, a left hander, who like McEnroe, also has tended to drag his game down by cynical behaviour. But he was hard to beat and very quick around court, pulling off devastating passing shots while running at top speed and full stretch along the baseline. Two years ago, the tall Lendl played his way to world No 1, at last gaining confidence in himself with his powerful passing shots down both wings and his strong service. But he lacked personality.

Of all these Borg did most for the game in behaviour and more than that, he was a standard-bearer who has been followed by young Swedish players like Wilander, Edberg, Jarryd and a fleet of others. Winners of the Davis Cup in 1984 and 1985 they are a world force at present.

Of women since the last war, Martina Navratilova, a Czech like Drobny in the 1950s and Lendl now, has been a dominating key figure of recent seasons. There are those who say that she could beat most men and here one would be inclined to agree, though not the leading men. She could have trouble in a fifth set. She is the third woman grand slam winner.

No-one can ignore little Billie-Jean King either, who looks like a bespectacled American college girl. She was extremely sharp in the volley, a natural all court player with considerable flexibility and fluency. Her Wimbledon record of twenty titles at singles, doubles and mixed doubles places her as one of the best all-round players of the past thirty or forty years.

Kitty would not have us forget the fine driving length, and overall control of little Maureen Connolly who was the first to achieve a woman's grand slam in 1953. With her nodding head she reminded one of a Japanese doll. Evonne Goolagong – later Mrs Cawley – was a very popular, artistic player who tended to lose concentration in the middle of a match but was a great competitor nonetheless.

With the mention of Connolly, Kitty also recalls the domination of Wimbledon by a quartet of American women – Louise Brough, Margaret Osborne (later Mrs Du Pont), Doris Hart and Shirley Fry. With Mrs Todd and Pauline Betz, they laid siege to the singles and doubles from 1946 to 1954. For nine years until the appearance of Maureen Connolly, they achieved what the French 'musketeers' had done in the 1920s. At that stage, for almost a decade, it was all Stars and Stripes. In 1948, in fact, Louise Brough played 117 games over three hours when competing in three matches on the final day.

It is odd that doubles have won less attention in the media and with crowds in general. Possibly it is lacking in the essential quality of a duel, a face to face challenge between two opponents alone on a stage; a question of character and fighting spirit. Yet in some ways there is more to doubles in tactics and teamwork. It is a game of geometrical angles, the reaction of two minds thinking as one, of instant reaction in defence and attack and the careful covering of a court. Speed of reflex is essential when all four players face each other at close range over a net. All this goes to make a fine doubles pair.

At times a barrage of close volleys can make doubles seem faster than singles; lobbing defensively from the back of the court when the opposition appear to control a rally often leads to the winning of an important point. And there is an Australian tactic – a tandem – now occasionally copied by others, where a partner at the net moves to the same court as his server, enticing an opponent to return service to the apparently open half of the court only to find his stroke cut off at the net by a swift volley. It is a clever move designed to put the opposition in two minds.

The only time Kitty has ever been involved in this Australian trick is when she played a doubles in retirement with her old friend, Jean Borotra. This variant tactic would obviously appeal to the eighty-nine years young mind of the Frenchman, even in a friendly! And despite winning 107 doubles titles in her tournament career Kitty was never involved in this clever tactic. She and her partners always 'played it straight' in the conventional, traditional way.

Pressed for her memories of doubles pairings, Kitty voted for Lenglen and Ryan as the best of the women's game. From 1919 to 1923 they won the title five years in succession and again in 1925 – six times in seven summers. It was during that run, in 1922, at the opening of the new Wimbledon, that Kitty, and her sister, Margaret, by then Mrs Stocks, met the formidable couple. When the sisters played together Margaret took the left hand court, very often the more difficult side. At one stage Margaret whispered to Kitty: 'If only I could take their bloody service I believe we would beat the favourites.' An understandable remark but the favourites won by 6–2, 6–4. Elizabeth Ryan was probably even ahead of Lenglen in the doubles game because of her volleying and overhead play.

Another good doubles player was Mrs Wightman of America, who created the Wightman Cup. She, too, volleyed and smashed well in partnership with Helen Wills. They won at Wimbledon in 1924 when Kitty again was on the losing side after her exciting singles win against Wills.

As Kitty said earlier, no-one can ignore the all-round ability of Billie Jean King in singles, doubles and mixed doubles. She won the doubles ten times between 1961 and 1979 and her best partner was little Rosemary Casals from San Francisco. Casals was a saucy player and a good volleyer.

Of the men, Kitty was impressed by Perry and Pat Hughes, always very sharp at the net, who brought the Davis Cup to Britain for four consecutive years. The Australian youngsters Hoad and Rosewall also took the eye with their mobility and good understanding. They had all the vitality of youth coupled with a shrewd instinct.

Kitty's finest mixed doubles win was in the semi final of the 1925 American championship. She and Jack Hawkes, an Australian, had lost the final of 1923 to Bill Tilden and Mrs Mallory. Two years later however they beat this formidable American pair to reach the final and lift the trophy.

There was a healthy playing relationship with her husband, Leslie Godfree, a Davis Cup player, with Kitty again playing in the forehand court to make maximum use of her forehand drive. Winners of the Wimbledon mixed in 1926 – a few months after their marriage – they are the only husband and wife to have lifted this mixed title.

Looking down the years it is interesting now how the patterns have been set and changed. In the 1920s it was the French who were in the driving seat through Lenglen and the Musketeers (Borotra, Cochet, Lacoste and Brugnon). They finally lost the Davis Cup to Britain, who could boast Perry, Bunny Austin, the first man to appear on the centre court in shorts, Pat Hughes and Tuckey. Since then Yvon Petra has been the only Frenchman to win the singles and also, in the first championship after the war, the last to wear long trousers.

After the decline of the French there came the United States with a powerful battery line of Budge, Ellsworth Vines in singles and the doubles partnerships of Allison and Van Ryn, and Van Ryn and Lott.

From the 1950s to the early 70s it was Australia, under the clever and strict guidance of Harry Hopman, who produced the cream at the top. Frank Sedgman led the way. Soon there followed a rich vein of champions – Lew Hoad, Ken Rosewall, and the young lions of Rod Laver, Ashley Cooper, Neale Fraser, Roy Emerson, John Newcombe and Tony Roche.

I saw the challenge round of the Davis Cup at Forest Hills in 1959 when Australia beat America by 3–2 with Fraser winning both his singles against Alex Olmedo and Barry McKay, and Laver, then at the beginning of his glittering career, losing both but helping Fraser to pull off the vital doubles.

Following Newcombe there has been an Australian decline with America again taking control through Stan Smith, McEnroe, Connors, Arthur Ashe and the doubles team of McEnroe and Fleming dominating all opposition.

More recently the pendulum has swung towards Europe. Czecho-slovakia, through Lendl, have put in a bid for the big prizes but at the time of writing it is Sweden who lead the way. Bjorn Borg's great success at Wimbledon inspired the whole country. Covered courts and coaching schools proliferated and there emerged a group of talented youngsters. West Germany made a spirited challenge in 1985 but they lacked a strong enough team to support young Boris Becker.

The curiosity is why Australia has not produced a string of first class women players. There has been the powerful Margaret Court, of course, and the largely unfulfilled promise of Evonne Cawley. Austra-lia has the climate, but so far only the men have regularly delivered. Special efforts have been made by all Australian state tennis associa-tions to train young players. Many leading women figures have been invited to contribute, but still the Americans lead the parade.

As a postscript, Kitty showed me an article on women players written by Bill Tilden in 1921. He had just won his second singles title at Worple Road on a visit from America so had only a brief view of the English game. Nonetheless his quick judgements are of interest:

Mrs Chambers is the 'Mavro' of women as regards her recovering ability. Her errors are reduced to a minimum at all times. To err is human; but at times there is something very nearly inhuman about Mrs Chambers' tennis.

Mrs Beamish – this English player is an exponent of the famous base-line game of the country. She drives along deep shots fore and backhand, corner to corner, chasing her opponent around the court for almost impossible distances. Her service, volleying and over-head are fair but not noteworthy. Another player of almost identical game and of almost equal class is Mrs Peacock, Champion of India. Her whole game is a little better rounded than Miss Beamish's, but she lacks the latter's experience.

The English-American star, Elizabeth Ryan, is another player of marked individuality. Born in California, Miss Ryan migrated to England while quite young. For the past decade 'Bunny', as she is called, has been a prominent figure in English and continental tournaments.

Miss Ryan has a queer push-reverse twist service that is well placed but carries little speed. She chops viciously forehand and backhand off the ground and storms the net at every opening. Her volleying is crisp and decisive. Overhead she is severe but erratic. She is a dogged fighter, never so dangerous as when behind. Her tactics are aggressive, attack at all times, but if this fails she is lost.

Although Miss Ryan is an American by birth she must be considered as an English player, for her development is due to her play in England.

Among the other women in England who are delightfully original in their games are Mrs Larcombe, the wonderful cut-stroke player, whose clever generalship and tactics place her in the front rank; Mrs McNair, with her volleying attack, and Miss K McKane, a young player of all-round excellence, potentially the best woman-player in England today.

Still a keen spectator of lawn tennis, and a shrewd television judge of cricket test matches and rugby football internationals, Kitty's interest in the passing scene is wondrous. To solicit her opinion of the past, its players and events, is to turn back the pages of history.

Within a short time of joining the tennis world she had become one of a 'gang of six' who fairly dominated the game. Those six who ruled the roost between 1919 and 1927 were the virtually unbeatable Suzanne Lenglen, of France, who became the ikon of the ladies' game from 1919 to 1925 with six All-England championship wins during those years; Helen Wills, the American, who won eight titles in twelve summers; Elizabeth Ryan, another senior American who had settled in

The McKane family: (1) Kitty's father, John

(2) Her mother, May

(3) With her sister, Margaret

(4) Kitty holds the St Leonards School lacrosse shield, about 1911

(5) Shows off her golf swing at St Andrews, at about the same time

(6) Poses for the cameras early in her tennis career

Two finals lost: (7) with Suzanne
Lenglen (rt) at Wimbledon in 1923

(8) With Helen Wills (rt) and American officials at the US
championships at Forest Hill in 1925

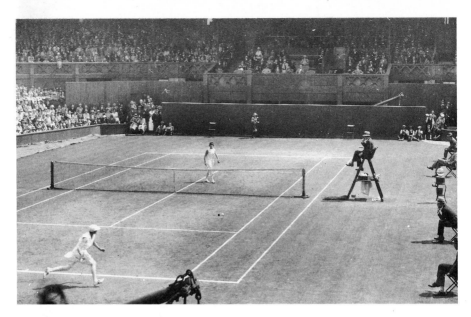

Double triumph: (9) In the 1924 Wimbledon final against Helen Wills (nearest the camera)

(10) With the 1925 Wightman cup team, who are (standing, left to rt) Joan Fry, Mr Batley (manager), Ermentrude Harvey, and (sitting) Kitty, Mrs Dorothea Lambert-Chambers (captain) and Evelyn Collyer.

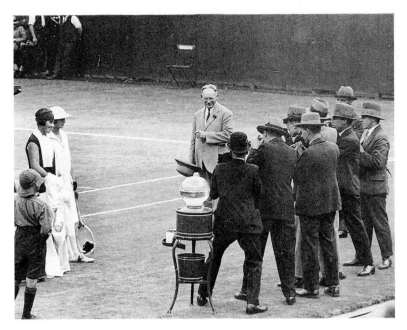

(11) Wimbledon winner, with Lili d'Alvarez in 1926

(12) Loser, to Helen Jacobs (rt) in 1931

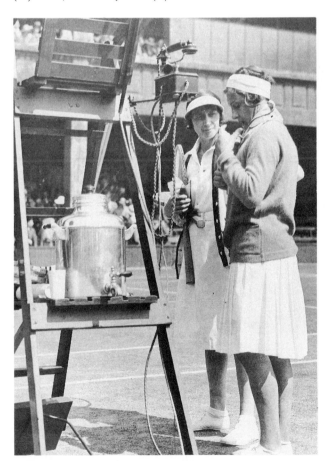

(13) Forehand drive: the stroke with which
Kitty Godfree wore down her opponents

(14) In a happy mood

(15) A happy pair: Leslie and Kitty at the
Wimbledon ball in the early fifties

(16) The author and Kitty at a joint birthday party at
Richmond in 1986

(17) A champion remembers: Kitty holds a quarter scale replica of the Wimbledon ladies salver, made for her in 1954 because in her day it was not allowed out of safekeeping; and the sculpture from the 1920 Olympics in Amsterdam

England in 1912 and gained nineteen doubles and mixed doubles titles in a distinguished career; Kitty herself with two titles from three finals, two mixed doubles wins, and a member of the only husband and wife partnership to lift the prize in 1926; Mrs Lambert Chambers, a dominating champion before the 1914 war who finally lost her crown to Lenglen in 1919; and Mrs Mallory, a former American title holder until Helen Wills came on the scene in 1923.

When Chambers and Mallory faded from the scene the young Spanish champion, Senorita Lili de Alvarez, joined the 'gang' having reached three consecutive finals in 1926, 1927 and 1928 only to lose them all. Her record can be compared with that of Ken Rosewall, the Australian, perhaps the best man, with Gonzales, not to have triumphed at Wimbledon in singles. After Senorita de Alvarez may be added the names of Dorothy Round and Helen Jacobs, who followed in the 1930s.

Of those in the 'gang' and of other great players Kitty has this to say:

SUZANNE LENGLEN

'Suzanne was queen of the 1920s. She was a wonderful player. She had obviously had dancing lessons in her youth and when she came to Worple Road for the first time in 1919, aged twenty, she immediately established herself as a prima ballerina. She had all the strokes, often played with both feet off the ground, which was natural, instinctive and not a question of showing-off.

'She hit hard, smashed, volleyed and was clever, accurate and concentrated with an all-round game which covered the length and breadth of the court. She could produce a top spin drive on both flanks, forehand and backhand, with an accurate serve which would swerve out of court pulling her opponent out of position. In a word she had finesse.

'I have often been asked how she compared with the stars of today. My answer is that the genius of one generation could be the genius of another. She had all the shots but, of course, the modern game is much faster, the equipment is so advanced in terms of rackets and balls and there is so much greater accent on fitness and training.

'Navratilova, for instance, has had a back-up team of a physiotherapist, a psychologist, a trainer and so on. Suzanne had none of this support. She played naturally and instinctively with only her father and sometimes her mother to accompany her on any travels. I believe that, after a year or so of modern training, Suzanne could lead the parade again if that were possible. This is a mtter of opinion and theory naturally. It is so difficult to judge one age with another.

'However, Suzanne did have a couple of flaws in her psyche. First, she was not a particularly fit or strong girl; she was temperamental and volatile and did not like being beaten which was about as frequent as a blue moon. Occasionally she lost a doubles but that virtually was all, apart from a singles in America when she pulled out of a second set through illness. That remains her only recorded defeat in a singles, if it can be regarded as a defeat.

'There were four controversial events in Suzanne's playing career and they need recording. The first incident came in 1924 at Wimbledon. Generally used to 6–0, 6–1, or 6–2 easy victories she was taken to a 6–4 hard third set before she could beat the shrewd American Elizabeth Ryan in a quarter final. But apparently she felt so drained by this match that she scratched from the semi-final to most people's surprise. As it happened it let me off the hook. I should have played her in that semi final and would probably have lost. In the event I received a walk over which let me into the final to beat Helen Wills for my first title.

'Next came an unfortunate incident in 1926 when the All England Club was celebrating its fiftieth birthday. All the champions past and present – the men's singles and doubles and the women's singles – were presented on the centre court to King George V and Queen Mary. The parade over, an exhibition women's doubles had been arranged on the centre court, of one set alone, to entertain the royal guests. Senorita Lili de Alvarez, the Spanish champion, had been paired with me to face a formidable partnership of Suzanne and Elizabeth Ryan.

'However, a couple of days earlier Alvarez had rung to say that she was not fit to take part and in her place was chosen a promising young Dutch player Miss Lea Bouman. This was billed as an exhibition match but by the time we had reached 5-all and 6-all the centre court crowd was in a state of great excitement. When the Dutch girl and I finally won 8–6, to tremendous applause, it was remarked that Suzanne hated to lose with a crowd against her.

'When she later scratched controversially from the third round no-one quite knew the reason. Was she truly unfit; was it the result of that exhibition doubles defeat earlier; or was it connected with an embarrassing misunderstanding with Queen Mary?

'I must say my sympathy was with Suzanne in this affair. Admittedly the original fault lay with her but it was undiplomatically dealt with by the Wimbledon referee, Mr Burrow. Every evening one had to report to him before going home to discover your programme for the next day. This Suzanne forgot to do.

'Next morning her doubles partner, Mlle Viasto, rang her hotel to ask if she knew she was due to play a singles before their doubles against Mrs Mallory and Mary Browne, a strong American pair. This news upset Lenglen who immediately rang her captain, Toto Brugnon, in another hotel, to complain at the order of play.

'Whether or not Toto got in touch with Wimbledon that morning is not clear. But Suzanne, due to play her single on court No 1 at two o'clock turned up at Wimbledon at half past three to run immediately into a storm. Burrow and the playing committee were furious; Suzanne said she preferred to play her difficult doubles first, followed by the single – in other words reverse the order – but Burrow would have none of it. He fumed that a wretched girl had been waiting on court No 1 for an hour and a half; the crowd was restive and in a bad temper and so on.

'He treated her like a naughty schoolgirl in a way that would never have happened in Paris or the South of France where she was the Queen. The merest diplomacy by Burrow could have saved the situation. By then the temperamental Suzanne, her hackles up, was in a towering rage. She withdrew to the ladies changing room with her mother. Both were in floods of tears; both were shouting, with Suzanne banging her fists on the walls and screaming.

'Jean Borotra entered our changing room and tried desperately to calm Suzanne with no result. Meanwhile, Queen Mary, who had arrived for tea, in time to see Lenglen and Vlasto play their doubles at five o'clock on the centre court, was kept waiting. Eventually Borotra, one of Mary's favourites, had to enter the royal box and tell the Queen that Suzanne was unwell and unable to play. The Queen accepted the apology and said she hoped Lenglen would get well. Suzanne's single and doubles were played the next day with a victory in each.

'That was that but Lenglen, who was due to be presented at court that summer by a titled English lady, learned that she had been quietly erased from the Buckingham Palace list.

'I think it was all mishandled at Wimbledon. What was needed was a bit of tact. Burrow was unprepared for French temperament from a girl who understood only basic English. A few days later came Suzanne's second withdrawal in three years which again let me through for a winning final against de Alvarez.

'It was round about 1927 when Helen Wills had begun her great run of eight singles titles that the United States Lawn Tennis Association suggested an exhibition match between Wills and Lenglen who, by then, had given up Wimbledon. It was no genuine exhibition, more of a challenge match between the States and France to prove who was the world champion.

'The French accepted and the meeting took place in the South of France – either Monte Carlo or Cannes – I can't exactly remember. Lenglen won by two sets to love whereupon the Americans invited Suzanne to appear in their championship at Forest Hills.

'Suzanne set out with her mother but they had a rough crossing of the Atlantic, which saw Suzanne very sick. They arrived in New York just in time before the championship started on the Monday. With no real time to settle down and practise, or to get the feel of the court at Forest Hills, Suzanne found that she had been drawn in the first round against Mrs Mallory who had been United States champion many times.

'Suzanne, obviously not fully recovered from her sea voyage lost the opening set but was leading 2–1 in the second when she approached the umpire to say that she was feeling unwell and would like to scratch. This, of course, became hot news everywhere and she became very unpopular with the American public who had wanted to see her probably get to the final and there be beaten by Helen Wills. Without further ado Suzanne took the next boat and headed for home. Thereafter she contented herself with exhibitions in her beloved South of France.

'There ended the tournament career of a glorious but controversial figure who not only set a new standard but who brought a new style in tennis clothes which the rest of the field were soon to follow.'

HELEN WILLS

'She became the American champion in 1923 at the age of seventeen. When I beat her in the Wimbledon final she was only eighteen and on her first visit to Europe. After that defeat she decided to keep away from Wimbledon for three years until 1927 when she felt she was ready to challenge. It was a wise move on her part since she took the title eight times in the next twelve summers.

'She learnt her game on Californian hard courts. A stylist, she was sound in her ground strokes but her real strength lay in service and a powerful forehand drive. She was no Lenglen, being somewhat mechanical with hard driving to a perfect length from the base line but a minimum of volleying. Even so she became very hard to beat, wearing down her opponent from long range. She was no runner but economical of movement, not unlike Mo Connolly later on in the 1950s. Maureen was a sweet young girl who was just beginning to add a volley to her game when a riding accident brought an end to her run of three titles of 1952, 53 and 54.

Helen, when I first met her socially, was very shy and quiet. Not a great conversationalist, which was understandable since she was still pretty young and a stranger to Europe. As I said she was no Lenglen; she was not the same delight to watch, but nonetheless she was a cut above the rest of us. Her results speak volumes.'

ELIZABETH RYAN

'Born in California four years before my own birth, Elizabeth settled in England in 1912. Known as Miss "chop and drop" she was a most skilful doubles player as her record reflects – twelve women's doubles and seven mixed doubles victories in the All-England championships – a total that was finally passed by Billie-Jean King in 1979, the same year as Elizabeth's death while watching the championships, at the age of eighty-seven.

'Though she never won the singles title she did reach the final twice, only to lose to Lenglen and Wills. She took Lenglen to a 6–4 hard third set in 1924 which caused the French champion to scratch from the semi final through exhaustion.

'Though basically a fearsome doubles opponent she was very hard to beat in a singles. This I discovered to my cost when I first started my round of domestic tournaments. I was continually running into her around the countryside. If my memory serves me now I think I lost six of our first seven meetings. I had to wait two years until I won at last – at Hendon in 1921 when I saved a match point in the second set and finally won 3–6, 7–5, 8–6.

'That was certainly a memorable victory for me. It gave me some confidence but it was not until 1922 that I could again beat her at Scarborough. When we both retired in the mid 1930s I was able to add up our meetings. Out of twenty-one contests I had won eleven to Elizabeth's ten, so that we were pretty well all square. She certainly had a head start on me but I caught her up in the end.

' "Chop and drop" was certainly an apt description of her play. The "chop" was an astute slice or spin played from the elbow (rather like a real tennis stroke) which often kept low and was cleverly placed; the "drop" was well disguised so that she kept you on the *qui vive*, uncertain what stroke to expect next. If I may use the expression it was often a match of "short-hand". She even had Lenglen guessing at times.

'At the beginning of my career in 1919 I suspect she regarded me as something of a young upstart who needed to be kept in her place, especially when I started to beat the pre-war top ladies who, of course, had lain fallow for over four years.

'Although unable to beat Lenglen or Wills, nevertheless she could boast being the singles title holder of nine countries and doubles champion of twenty-two. Her most interesting win was in St Petersburgh in 1914 when the Czar was still on the throne. The prize looked like a silver tea kettle which can now be seen in the Wimbledon museum.

'Her greatest claim was: "I am the shrewdest picker of doubles partners in the world"; she once played with the King of Portugal at Queens Club. Her greatest admiration was invested on Lenglen. "Suzanne" she said, "had a stride a foot and a half more than most people. No wonder she got up to the net so quickly." '

Elizabeth Ryan achieved something in the championships that has lived on in legend – as long as any of her great achievements as doubles partner with Suzanne Lenglen. There was a special quality about it and showed both considerable quality of character and disregard for popular opinion. During a singles match at Worple Road, shortly after the first world war, she suspended play after a rally on a hot and sultry day to remove her stays on court. Causing shock and surprise to some spectators she was admired by many for her honesty of purpose in a most uncomfortable situation!

DOROTHEA LAMBERT CHAMBERS

'Dorothea undoubtedly was the mistress of pre-war tennis, winning the All-England title seven times from 1903 to 1914. Born in 1878 she was eighteen years older than myself yet was still playing after the war in 1919.

Although forty-one years of age she came nearest to a singles victory over Lenglen in England. In the 1919 final she held two match points against the young French genius in the third and final set. She only lost by a whisker.

'First Suzanne rescued a lob recovering the ball off the wood just over the net 30–40. Chambers serving. Then Dorothea placed a fore-hand drive two inches into the tramlines with Suzanne nowhere near the shot: deuce. Reprieved, Lenglen won her first title by 10–8, 4–6, 9–7.

'Although lacking in severity and possessing an excellent volley Dorothea was a baseline player. She was very good at the smash and was one of the few before the war to serve overarm. She was also very active, very steady and could produce an accurate lob at the right moment.

'Despite her distinguished past (she was also in four losing finals, the last against Lenglen in 1920) she was a very kindly person whom I sometimes partnered in doubles, but oddly enough we never met in singles so far as I can remember.'

MRS MALLORY

'Molla Mallory had been champion of the United States for some time until the crown went to Helen Wills. That was in singles but she remained very good at doubles and joined Bill Tilden as a mixed partnership. It was this frightening pair that John Hawkes, the Austra-lian, and I beat in the semi final at Boston to win the United States mixed in 1925.

'Molla, like many in those days, was essentially a baseline operator, and she was always hard to beat. We had some good tussels in the early Wightman Cups series. She volleyed little, if at all, but she was a canny placer of the ball and lobbed well.

'She beat me fairly easily in the first Wightman Cup in 1923 when Forest Hills was opened and Great Britain was white-washed 7–0. But I got my revenge in the Wimbledon Wightman tie in 1924 and again in 1925 when we won at Forest Hills by 4–3. I feel I made my mark when I beat her in the second round at Wimbledon by 6–1, 6–0 the year I won the title. On that occasion it was my non-stop volley attack that dominated her.'

SENORITA LILI DE ALVAREZ

'Everybody loved Lili. She was different from one or two others who were mere pot hunters. Lili was as charming as her name, playing joyously for the pure love of the game. Quite apart from her tennis, she was an all-round girl, excelling at fencing and ice skating.

'She was a very distinguished Spanish lady and a most charming and attractive figure to grace the centre court. She had a devil-may-care style with excellently produced strokes. Younger than most of us she was very sporting and carefree. Artistic and attractive, one of her unusual strokes was the half volley sometimes played far back in court, near the baseline. This saved the effort of running and almost matched the half-volley ability of Henri Cochet who could pick up a ball off his shoe laces. Champion of Spain, it was a pity she could never quite capture the Wimbledon crown.'

DOROTHY ROUND

'Although champion in 1934 and 1937 one of the oddities of her game was inexplicable nerves. They were as difficult to conquer as her opponent. But once mastered in a match she could play with a series of lovely flowing ground strokes. She could also volley and serve well.

'Dorothy was also a formidable doubles player, but even then with someone to talk to on court – which she missed in a singles when she felt lonely – her nerves tended to make her dithery. Once playing a doubles with her she suddenly appealed to me: "Biddy, would you take all the smashes. I know I'll make a mess of them and the others are rather good." I replied: "Don't be silly Dorothy. We're already a set up and leading again. Besides which we're rather good, too." But still Dorothy left me to do the work overhead.

'I, myself, was sometimes a slow, uncertain starter, but I never suffered like Dorothy.'

HELEN JACOBS

'Champion in 1935 but beaten in five other finals the two Helens, Wills and Jacobs, were close rivals. Jacobs the younger of the American pair, had a greater range and variety of strokes but just lacked the power of Wills. She had a good all-round game to make a match of it. Later on the unfortunate Helen Jacobs suffered from poor health.'

ALICE MARBLE

'Like Lenglen, Alice was the epitome of grace. All her strokes were played with fluent ease and at times she could hit the ball harder than any woman of her era. A marvellous all-rounder, she could serve, and volley with speed and accuracy and could control a match tactically. Her one fault was to try to hit the cover off the ball.

'After the ladies champions parade on the centre court in 1984, she and I were interviewed by BBC radio at a studio beneath the royal box. She had been coaching in California for the past forty years; she proved very articulate and certainly outshone me. She is greatly to be admired for having had the willpower to overcome a serious illness. Tennis could have done with more of her.'

'So much for some of the leading women players between the wars. Since 1946, of course, tennis as a whole has changed into a top gear. It is now in overdrive. Money and materialism have taken over and much of the early fun has gone out of the game. It is all so much more serious and the players work that much harder to gain the rich prizes. Yet there are some who provide first class entertainment. Amongst these I would place the following:

MARIA BUENO

'The first Brazilian girl to win the singles title she was a lovely looking person with a game to match her looks. She served well, volleyed superbly with killing angles, and had a fluent all-court game that dominated the stage. She was quite regal, straight backed and upright. She won in 1959, 1960 and 1964, but lost to Margaret Smith (later Court) and Billie-Jean King in 1965 and 1966. When she returned to Sâo Paulo after her initial victory she returned a heroine to the extent that the Brazilians erected a statue of her in her home town, and presented her with a motor car, I also heard she had been given a helicopter, but this I can't vouch for.'

ALTHEA GIBSON

'For the two years before Bueno had come the athletic Althea Gibson, the first black player to win at Wimbledon. She was very lithe, swift to volley and quick to anticipate. She was tall, had all the strokes and was exciting to watch. Very flexible, she was also good at netball and, I believe, joined the famous Globe Trotters team who were visiting entertainers in many countries.'

'Nearer to our day are five women who have mostly become millionairesses as they fought their way out of the pack. They are *Martina Navratilova, Chris Lloyd, Hana Mandlikova, Billie-Jean King* and *Mrs Margaret Smith (Court)*.

'I really don't have to talk much about these since they are in the forefront of all tennis fans' eyes. All I would add is that they are very well behaved in both victory and defeat with Chrissie showing an ice-cool exterior whether winning or losing. Chrissie's great shot is the two-handed backhand, hit with power and precise enough to thread the eye of a needle. Basically she is a baseliner, yet can volley when she has to and has developed a clever masked drop shot.

'Two of the others are Czech born, though Martina had since become a naturalised American. She is a superbly athletic volleyer and smasher, strong enough to have recently achieved the first ladies grand slam since Margaret Smith in 1970.

'It was following my presentation of the winning gold plate to Navratilova at the end of her fifth consecutive title victory over young Hana Mandlikova in the finals last summer (1986), that Martina and I were required to appear on television face to face.

'During this interview it was Martina, who proposed a match against myself. "Don't be silly, my dear. It would be a waste of your time. You're much too strong and fit. You're in a different world." "If you say so," replied Martina. "Anyway, let's have a knock-up. I'll play lefthanded!" "No, I don't think so," I replied. "Better still, let me partner you in a doubles!" she rejoined. There we left it amid some friendly laughter.

'Of the group little Mandlikova to me is the most impressive. Although without the vast stride of Margaret Court or the telling volleying finesse of Billie-Jean she has a fine balanced movement and many attractively produced strokes. Her one weakness is a sudden loss of concentration as she goes "walkabout" inexplicably to lose a few games in the middle of a match. However, as 1985 champion of America, she may redress this fault with a gain of confidence.'

11

Contrasts – Past and Present

Kitty, who has lived through five reigns, now wears trousers as she cycles to morning shopping, something which would doubtless have shocked the opinion of her Victorian mother and father. Yet life is all about change, and Kitty is very much a part of the process in the latter part of the twentieth century.

But there are certain qualities that do not, or should not, alter. And it is to these that older generations still cling – abstracts such as good behaviour, manners, and sportsmanship. These were collectively described as the Corinthian spirit. Sadly there is not much evidence of that same spirit today. But let us now question Kitty on some of the changes that have enveloped tennis in her life, beginning with the issue of behaviour.

BEHAVIOUR

'I can't remember any rows in our day – certainly nothing like the fracas that blow up nowadays. There *might* have been a McEnroe amongst us but he knew that if he showed his face or raised his voice in protest that would have been the end of him in the tennis circle. He would have been blackballed and immediately sent packing.

'Modern players may think we were spiritless "namby-pambies" but we played under a strict discipline which has disappeared these days. The behaviour of some players now is disgraceful and sadly some sections of the crowds seem to encourage and enjoy these outbursts. It is my humble opinion that fellows like McEnroe, Nastase, Connors, and one or two others should have been disqualified at times and even denied entry to certain tournaments. But committees have been weak, with an eye on the gate money that might have been lost by the absence of such stars.

'Yet I wonder if these officials were, or are, right. I seem to remember that when Pilic, the Yugoslav, was suspended by the International Lawn Tennis Federation in 1973, nearly eighty players withdrew from Wimbledon under instructions from the Association of Tennis Professionals. It was a political strike which could never have existed in our day. But in spite of the absence of all these big names the Wimbledon crowds still attended in their thousands.

'The fundamental trouble is the vast prize money now available. A single wrong call by a linesman could cost thousands of dollars which sparks all the misbehaviour and obscene language. There are certain points penalties that can be imposed by an umpire but these are largely inadequate.

'The damage is reflected in youth who are always keen to follow and imitate the stars. This hardly augurs well for the future. I read of some youngster in an important youth tournament in Europe who hit his opponent over the head with his racket. Heaven help us if the equivalent of soccer violence should invade tennis.'

TIE-BREAK SYSTEM

'This has been one of the most sensible and acceptable changes in the last twenty years. It was introduced in 1971, a couple of years after Gonzales and Pasarell had stretched a match on the centre court to 112 games over two or three days of weather interruptions. Some may have found this exciting: others a boring marathon.

'In a sense it is not unlike Russian roulette which I believe came from an American, Jimmy van Alen, who tried to alter the scoring of tennis. Out of his strange deliberations came this system of the tie-break which I believe has been a great success. It saves exhaustion and can help to decide a match by skill rather than the extremes of fitness.

'More than that it is something of a social asset. For instance, there are those who buy expensive seats for the centre or No 1 court in the expectation of seeing a good ladies' singles or doubles but instead are glued to their posts having to watch two men's matches each of which could last three to four hours. And this is to the exclusion of the ladies who can't get on court.

'The most exciting tie-break I can remember – one that was neither sharp nor quick – was between Borg and McEnroe in the final, I think, of 1980. I believe it lasted for something like thirty-four points.'

PRESS AND TELEVISION

'There was no television until 1937 when transmission took place from the centre court. Thus we were not invaded or troubled by this new wonder. Of course television now helps to promote and popularise the game with its excellent camera work and its slow motion repeats. This shows the value of great stroke play. In many ways in fact one can see the close-up reaction of players far better than sitting some way from the play. Watching a match live, of course, does involve one in the atmosphere but even here the camera on screen can reflect the live involvement.

'But one thing I would blame it for is the blowing up of rows and arguments which many grown-ups think unseemly and which set a bad example for youngsters. I think this is a mistake. I imagine rows have to be recorded since it is both a fact of life and news worthy, but to dwell too long on them is an error of judgement about which I think producers or directors should think seriously. Unfortunately there are some people in a crowd who enjoy these explosive moments. It is theatre to them, part of their nature. They are the sort of people who like seeing rebellious crowds fighting with the police.

'Newspapers, too, the tabloid variety in particular, seem to lick their lips over a row involving a linesman or an umpire. At such moments the cameramen descend like vultures to record the scene. After matches most of the leading players are interviewed by the press and sometimes questions are asked of a personal nature, about a girl friend or a wife, which upsets the player and a crude argument can ensue. These correspondents are usually in search of a "scoop", backed up by news reporters who see little or nothing of the tennis but search for backstage stories. There are only a handful of correspondents the players trust.

'Luckily we did not have to suffer such a corps of newshounds. There were no backroom stories for anyone and if one appeared in print it was the work of a Hans Anderson. We were the relics of the Victorian and Edwardian ages. Life had not gained the speed of today. We were shy, well behaved and, I suppose, rather colourless – except, of course, Suzanne Lenglen, the French orchid, who quite apart from her tennis, was a leader of tennis fashion.

'Just imagine what modern reporters would have done about her withdrawals from the championships of 1924 and 1926. And what a field day they would have had with the misunderstanding with Queen Mary. They would probably have had England and France at war.

'Our writers were descriptive. Tennis was their job and they stuck to their subject. The only ones I really remember were Stanley Doust of the *Mail* and Wallis Myers of *The Daily Telegraph*. Both had been players and they knew what they were writing about. I enjoyed reading them.

'What really irritated us in those days were the photographers. That was at Worple Road. There were not many of them but they used to cluster near the side lines. Their cameras were of an old fashioned type, not like the modern Swiss and Japanese equipment. They had to use plates for their photos and every time they took a picture the heavy plate would drop making a disturbing noise. This would put us off when playing a stroke near the side lines, never knowing, but half expecting, the noise of a falling plate.

'We used to complain as gently as possible and got them pushed away from the lines. The players of today are similarly distracted by clicks and flash bulbs, but today's complaints are rather more vociferous than ours. I sympathise with the modern player in this instance.'

LINESMEN

'Linesmen were not as well organised then as now. Before and just after the first war it was all very amateur and hit or miss. In the provincial, domestic tournaments for example the players themselves were often called upon for this duty, to run a line as well as possible. But there was no-one to sit near the net post with a hand on the net to detect a net call for service. That was left to the judgement of the players themselves. And since the rules said that 'play should be continuous' there was no rest at the change of ends and no seats to take a ninety second breather as today.

'Frankly I have a great respect for the present linesman. He is like the wretched soccer referee and linesmen who are the aunt sallies of the crowds. The modern official needs to have eyes like a hawk to cope with the speed of the game. Certainly he has some help from the 'Cyclops', the electronic eye that deals with the flashing service, indicating a fault with a bleep. But even that is not always foolproof.

'It is a great strain to be on the line particularly with such vast sums of prize money at stake. The nervous strain, as well as eye strain, is very wearing. The umpires and linesmen these days have an association, so much better organised than their predecessors. Now a team of fresh linesmen take over from those on the lines of a match every forty-five minutes. It is rather like the changing of the guard or the rest given to aircraft pilots.

'Linesmen can, of course, be overruled by the umpire. There was an occasion when Helen Wills had challenged Suzanne Lenglen in an exhibition match in the South of France around 1926 which I mentioned earlier. It was a two-set match and Suzanne, having won the opener, stood at match point in the second. She drove down the side line and since it all appeared finished the large crowd cheered wildly. But an Englishman, Lord Charles Hope, was on that line and he had to run to the umpire to say that he had called the shot out but because of the cheering no-one had heard him. At this there was a bit of a storm and Suzanne, reduced to deuce, had to win two more rallies for the match.

'There was another occasion at the Wimbledon centre court when Brigadier Jackie Smyth VC was on the base line for a doubles. He told me this story himself. Apparently he had snoozed off in the sunshine when he awoke to see a ball land in the tramlines. He immediately called a fault thinking it was a service. In fact it was a rally and was a winning stroke. Swiftly realizing his mistake he turned and glared daggers at a man sitting in the front row of the spectators. Everyone then thought it was the spectator who had called, a let was allowed, and Smyth got away with his error. You would expect such quick thinking from a VC!

'Another incident, a sad one, concerned a lady linesman on court No 3, in the 1960s (I think). Again it was a hot, sunny afternoon. After a set or two the dear lady suddenly fell off her chair. It transpired that she was tiddly and had fallen into a deep sleep. Naturally there was nothing else to do but lead her away and produce a replacement. All this was meat and drink to the news reporters and I imagine she suffered a shaming time when she saw the next day's newspapers.

'My husband, Leslie, was president of the Umpires Association and he had the unpleasant duty of telling her that her services were no longer required. I only mention this unfortunate affair because the lady in question has since moved on to the supreme referee in the sky.

'But there were those who blamed the All-England Club for giving a drinks party before play instead of at the end of the day!

'As for umpires there will be three full time professionals amongst them this summer travelling the world for all the Grand Prix events.'

YOUNG BEGINNERS

'Not before time the international authority has realised the harm being done to the young who tend to be pushed by greedy parents with the vision in their eyes of the silver dollar. It is like trying to put one's daughter on the stage to be a Shirley Temple. They take no notice of Noel Coward's song: "Don't put your daughter on the stage Mrs Worthington."

'There have been tournaments for under 12s and under 14s – even, I understand, under 10s! These, I believe, are being rightly outlawed because of the alarm at the growing casualty lists of these youngsters who are being exhausted and burnt out mentally and physically by the strains imposed.

'Tracy Austin, of America, who threatened to become another Mo Connolly and who became a millionairess at seventeen and Andrea Jaeger, an equally young talent, three or four years ago, have both been affected by the stress and for the time being have dropped out of the picture.

'There are other fledglings like Gabriela Sabatini, a seventeen year old Argentinian, the eighteen year old Steffi Graf, of West Germany, and Carling Bassett, of Canada, who have already tasted the tension and pressures of Wimbledon. They are all charming and trim, but what are the fires burning within and how long will they last?

'It is very sad. The morning dawn of childhood, with its delicate bloom, its clear pure light, its joy of innocence and expectation has been left behind. True, in 1887 the athletic Lottie Dod, of Great Britian, became the youngest winner of the Wimbledon women's singles at the age of fifteen. But that virtually was the dawn of creation with only some twenty women in the field.

'I think they should be fifteen before they are influenced by coaches.

'There is one special case I should like to mention. He is the young German, Boris Becker, who won the men's singles in 1985. It was a remarkable achievement. Aged seventeen, unseeded, he fought his way through the pack with his energetic lust for life. He was vivacious and happy.

'Soon enough he was snapped up by the Rumanian Tiriac – some time ago a doubles partner of Nastase – as manager of his future. Immediately he was thrown into more deep water, in America, and Australia. Though he did well in the Davis Cup final in Germany against Sweden he got beaten by a variety of good players but not Wimbledon champions. This was last year when I understand his food diet was being changed. His vivacity had gone and he seemed disconnected.

'That was in 1985. Last summer (1986) he proved me wrong. His vivacity returned, he served magnificently again and he retained his Wimbledon title. Aged eighteen he would reign for some time, but should McEnroe return to find his old form that would be Becker's test.'

CROWDS AT THE CHAMPIONSHIPS

'Although I was not there, of course, I have read that 200 spectators, paying a shilling each, watched the first All England final of 1877. Nowadays the aggregate attendance for the meeting has never fallen below 300,000 since 1973 with a record of 358,000 in 1981. The annual profit from 1976 to 1980 was in the region of £350,000. These are figures to make the mind boggle.

'On the whole the crowds are well enough behaved. The main area where police are active is outside the Doherty Gates (East) and the Perry Gates (West) where they are occupied dealing with ticket touts who need to make a "killing" during the fortnight but are now prosecuted.

'There used to be long queues to see Suzanne Lenglen, the four French musketeers of Borotra, Cochet, Lacoste and Brugnon, and the great American Bill Tilden. But that was nothing like today, though in earlier times the gathering used to be more fashionable.

'Now those who queue on the Thursday, Friday, Saturday and Sunday of the second week – the last four days of the championship – have to possess tickets, even for standing room. For the rest of the fortnight it is first come, first served apart from club members and those with seat tickets.

'Even the worst weather does not deflect the hardy British. Huge queues spill out along the East and West pavements, many of them having slept out the night. As at awkward interviews and sprint races, the start is everything. The thing is to get in on the ground floor, to acquire a vantage point and avoid being poised like a gull on a cliff side. There is considerable enthusiasm. The people want to feel a part of the rallies, the vast rewards and the arguments.

'Certain people in the surrounding residential areas have sold up and moved away, stifled by the Wimbledon hordes; others have turned the championship fortnight into a money making affair, offering parking spaces in their front gardens for motor cars. Even here inflation has risen sharply in recent years. There was none of this at Worple Road.

'What was more in evidence then were top hats and Ascot fashion for the ladies. But basically crowds of today are much the same a those of yesterday. It is the British players who receive the greatest support.'

COACHES

'I was never coached. What ability I may have had was natural and instinctive. In any case there was little or no coaching in my day and I imagine none at all before the first war in the days when women served underarm. The first woman to serve overarm is buried in the mists of time although it may have been the athletic fifteen year old Lottie Dod who won the singles title five times before the turn of the century.

'The only advice – not coaching – I got was from uncles and cousins when I first picked up a racket at the age, I suppose of ten. 'Use your right hand' they used to urge. 'Tennis is played with the right hand.'

'So right hand it became. Yet basically I am left handed. I used to play cricket left handed, as batsman, bowler, fielder and thrower; I was left handed at lacrosse; I serve cards and write left handed. I now wonder if I would have done better on my natural, port side. Because of my tennis I played badminton with the right hand. This cannot now be answered, but sometimes I wonder.

'I suppose coaching can be useful in the modern game yet I feel it is overdone. It may help to strengthen certain weaknesses, but it tends to make some players rather regimental and limits natural flair.

'Perhaps it might have improved my play, but not having been taught and relying on whatever natural ability I had I am not enthusiastic about coaching. Perhaps this is one of my blind spots along with promoters, managers, agents and publicity men. No doubt they all need to earn a living but to me they seem to be limpets on the backs of the big fish. I feel that tennis should be taken by the feet, turned upside down, and shaken free of some of these parasites.'

LAW CHANGES

'The foot fault law is rather technical. What I would say is that it was stricter in my day when we had to assume a rigid stance on the serving base line. A change in the law now allows players a freedom to approach the net far faster after a service. Fred Perry tells me it allowed him to deliver faster and get to the net quicker.'

WOMEN IN TENNIS

'As for equal pay for women, I sympathise with their struggle for bigger prizes. Billie-Jean King and Ann Jones have worked hard and well to improve conditions for the girls. This may seem strange coming from someone who was happy enough to receive £5 vouchers for a win in the old days. I think they have made a mark when there are all-ladies tournaments as at Eastbourne just before Wimbledon. They can provide some fine, exciting matches and much to the point, women generally behave themselves.

'No doubt there are those who will accuse me of being a tennis suffragette and point me to the opinion of the late, great Elizabeth Ryan who said that women did not play five sets. "Let them face men," she remarked in a voice to silence further argument.'

12

O d d s   a n d   E n d s

Neither money nor silver trophies were a spur to Kitty. To her the real spur was the fun and enjoyment to be had from a game – any game. She always played to win, of course, but win, lose or draw it was the total joy to be had that mattered. Her attitude embodied the Olympic oath – it was the taking part that truly mattered. She had the reputation of being a strong finisher and I believe it was this spirit that saw her so often turn apparent defeat into victory at the last breath.

That she was never a pot hunter was proved when I asked her to talk of some of her most precious prizes. What intrigued me was the fact that her drawing room, though very comfortable and homely, was singularly bereft of medallions. Anyone who had won as many tournaments over the years would surely have had glass cases filled with silver and gold trinkets. But no. All Kitty rather shyly could point to was a miniature replica of the gold plate now presented to a women Wimbledon singles champion and to a handsome Waterford cut glass vase.

In her day all the Wimbledon winner received was a £5 voucher through the post; the miniature replica standing on a consul table was a gift from her solicitor husband Leslie. One day in the 1950s he had said to her: 'I've just made a killing on the stock exchange. Would you like a replica of the ladies' gold plate?' 'Yes, I think so,' she replied. Whereupon he made arrangements with the Wimbledon authorities who undertook the commission. But he had to pay for it of course.

The Waterford glass vase was a presentation by the Duke and Duchess of Kent to every surviving singles winner at the 1984 centenary of the Women's Championship – begun in 1884 – held on the centre court. So in a sense both these trophies are retrospective. 'But where are all the others?' I asked. 'Mostly up in the attic, I think, wrapped in newspaper,' was the vague reply. There is a recent photograph of her taken in her garden. On her right-hand side sits the miniature replica. Held in her left hand is a model of a male figure. Obviously it is a prize won, probably abroad, possibly Olympic, but she has no idea what it is. This amply sums up her view of materialism.

But the biggest shock for me came over her Olympic medals. The last two Olympics including tennis were held at Antwerp in 1920 and Paris in 1924. In those two tournaments Kitty had collected, in all, five medals – one gold, two silver and two bronze. Now she has not one of them. Others would surely have had them prominently displayed.

'You see, almost immediately after the first world war, I started travelling the countryside playing tournaments. I had no home of my own; I lived with my parents but had little space to store things. They moved two or three times, flat to flat, and took my things, with them. I imagine these Olympic medals were with them each time they moved, but somehow they either got lost on the way or were pinched by the furniture removers.'

I knew exactly what she meant. How often had similar things happened to oneself. 'It was a shame,' she continued, 'but I once found myself in an embarrassing position. I was invited to a British Olympic dinner. When the speeches got under way there came a call for medal winners to stand up to be applauded. When the gold winners were called – chaps like Harold Abrahams who had beaten the Americans at 100 metres – I sat firm and never moved. The same for the silver. But when the call for bronze came I plucked up courage and stood. I felt I deserved a third place. Earlier I had felt guilty with nothing, no medals or anything as proof. It was really rather silly of me. I was shy I suppose. But thinking about it now I realise they wouldn't have invited me in the first place.'

But one rather handsome item hangs in Kitty's sitting room. Well framed, it is a portrait of her in tennis clothes painted by Sidney White after her 1924 victory over Helen Wills. No-one commissioned it and the family, rather hard up after the war, never acquired it. It was painted and then just disappeared with the artist, Kitty never gave it another thought.

Then a strange thing happened. In the late 1970s, when the Wimbledon museum had been decided upon, two or three people were hunting around for memorabilia and artifacts. One of them, Max Robertson, of BBC radio, came across a painting in a back room of an antique shop. He phoned Tony Cooper, who had been appointed curator of the intended museum, to view the discovery. 'Oh yes. That's Kitty all right.' So fifty years later the painting reappeared.

Now there is a special arrangement with Wimbledon. It hangs in Kitty's drawing room, but at the end of every May she returns it to the museum for public view and they then return it to her when the Wimbledon fortnight is over. It is a generous arrangement, 'on loan to the champion for life'.

It is extraordinary how things suddenly turn up. Last year Sotheby's announced that a large painting had come to hand for auction at a reserve price of £8000 to £12,000. It was a painting of the centre court with its packed audience watching the final of 1923 between Kitty and Suzanne Lenglen. The artist was Miss M Watherston, the sale was on May 21 of last summer. The museum knew of it but decided not to bid. It duly went for a price of just over £23,000!

At the start of the second world war Kitty and her family headed west to the area of Bideford before the bombing started. It is a lovely area which they were to visit often in the years to come. Often there was an adventure of one sort or another.

Once they were staying at an attractive old farm in the area where they knew the owner very well. One day she said to Kitty that the place was haunted and asked if she had been disturbed by anything strange. The ghost, it appeared, was an old farmer who had lived there several hundred years earlier.

What he did apparently was to beat his walking stick on the door of the room where Kitty slept with her younger son. He would then shimmer through the room, and through the wall leading to the next bedroom where the elder son David slept on his own. This would happen around 4.00 am and the conclusion was that he was waking up his farm hands with his stick to get the day started.

Kitty and the boys never saw anything unusual but some years later they heard from the lady that her maid had abandoned her through fright and she herself had moved to another house. The ghost had become very violent by then and she had arranged with the Bishop of Exeter to exorcise the building. That had a calming effect and the ghost had vanished.

On another occasion in 1941 around the Bideford area Kitty and the boys joined up with a schoolgirl friend of hers, Billie Skipwith, who had come with her sister from London to St Leonards School at St Andrews. For thirty years they had kept in touch with each other.

On this occasion, David, by now eleven years of age, had bought a canoe for five shillings but before being allowed to take it on the water he had to pass a test given by 'Aunt' Billie to him and her daughter Wendy. She would take them out in her boat and suddenly push them both overboard into the River Torridge. Dressed in sweaters and gumboots they had to swim. Having proved that they could do so, David was allowed into his canoe and Wendy into hers.

David used to moor his boat on the foreshore and one morning when he went to launch it into the Torridge he found it stuck by what at first he thought was a log of wood. On close inspection, however, he discovered it was a dead German in a field grey flying uniform. Obviously he had been shot down and been in the water some time.

Leaving his younger brother Martin on guard, David ran like a scalded cat into the village to a house called 'Springfield' where an officer and troop of Royal Engineers were billeted. David roused an officer but it took three or four cross examinations before the officer decided it was time for him to investigate. Off he went, leaving David behind, upset at not being allowed to have another look. It caused quite a stir in the village and proved a good story to dine out on.

Once, on a certain holiday in Switzerland in the 1930s Leslie, who was never at home on skis – unlike Kitty – had a number of falls on the nursery slopes. He really became fed up to the back teeth and talked about going home. Until one day.

He was just about to try the slopes one last time when a German and his wife started a conversation near him. Obviously the man was giving his wife instructions and confidence. Eventually with a barrage of 'Ya, Ya's' the wife took a deep breath and set forth down the slope to her destiny. Miraculously she got to the bottom without a fall or a hiccup of any sort.

Having achieved her goal there was great excitement and celebration. She stood at the bottom waving her arms joyously and repeating her barrage of 'Ya's'. The husband likewise waved and shouted.

This was too much for Leslie. Turning to Kitty he said in a strangled voice: 'If that ruddy housefrau can do it, so shall I.' There was a steely look about him as he prepared to take off.

By some miracle he reached the bottom unscathed for the first time and home was forgotten temporarily. Kitty got an extra week's holiday because of that frau!

13

A Lively Retirement

The last tournament Kitty took part in was the covered court championship at Queen's Club in October 1935, when, aged thirty-nine, she reached the doubles semi final partnered by Susan Noel. Half a century has passed since Kitty struck her last stroke publicly, yet she still hit a tennis ball with friends once or twice a month in the covered courts of her beloved Wimbledon, until last year, her ninetieth.

Her energy is astonishing, especially in springtime and summer when she is constantly on the go, gardening, cutting the grass, playing bridge, visiting friends, shopping daily on her bicycle for the family and lunching every Sunday with colleagues at her favourite club, Wimbledon.

Most women in their nineties now would be found sitting quietly at home, probably watching television or reading, if their eyesight was up to it. They may be dependent on the social services in a variety of ways as they live out their old age. No-one can accuse Kitty of this. Few, if any, cracks have begun to show. It was really rather awkward talking to her about retirement. The word is not included in her vocabulary. In 1984 there was that trip to the Los Angeles Olympics, with Basil Hutchins, as representatives of the Wimbledon championships. It was a journey that would have worn out most people half her age. Don't be surprised should she go to Seoul in South Korea for the tennis Olympics tournament of 1988.

What keeps her so wound up is the interest she shows in most things – except 'Pop' which she finds an assault on her eardrums. Kiri Te Kanawa or Pavarotti are more her mark. Sewing was a pleasant diversion at one time until the family grew up, as was cooking for a healthy family with large appetites. Even now, rain, snow or shine, she cycles four or five times a week with shopping lists for the family and even neighbours. Her own tastes do not include beef or most meats, apart from chicken and tasty lamb chops. Slim and wiry, her weight is around eight and a half stone, which explains her vitality and energy.

A quiet game of croquet, either at Wimbledon or Hurlingham, often leads to tea and cucumber sandwiches to bring an echo of the old days, but it is sport on television that often keeps her on the edge of her seat. She cannot understand why so many rugby penalty kicks are conceded close in front of the posts and argues the point with any young rugby players she meets. But what really riles her is the West Indian fast bowling which threatens the batsman's body rather than his stumps. 'It is not cricket,' she says. 'The West Indian umpires should have put a curb on it.'

Her recent performance was to play against an American veterans team at Wimbledon and win both her doubles matches which astonished everyone. Recently, too, she has been elected patron of the British Veterans Lawn Tennis Club of which Leslie Godfree was a President and a founder member.

What makes it all work is her alertness of mind. She is very interested in politics. While by nature a 'leftie' at sport she leans to the right wing in politics and applauded the United States for their air raid on Libya, for they at least, she insisted, had tried to answer terrorism. She has even attended political meetings during elections with friends and neighbours who have 'heckled' speakers. She enjoys the rough and tumble of it all, just as she enjoys the mental challenges of bridge.

Her reading tastes tend towards excitement, not pure blood and thunder, but novels with a lively, compulsive plot. She has tasted Doris Lessing and Iris Murdoch and Wilbur Smith. But her real favourites are the 'whodunits' of Agatha Christie and the intriguing themes of racing by the ex-jockey, Dick Francis. She claims she has read all his books.

Mention of horses took her back to days of childhood, to Henley on Thames, where the family owned a pony and trap. The pony, named Dickie, happened to be rather lazy, often stopping on the way to the station to indulge in a roadside munch of grass. Her father used to get slightly tired of these delays and found an answer to them. At the bottom of their garden ran a bubbling, cold stream which joined the

Thames. It was into the water that the pony would be made to walk before a journey to sharpen him up. They loved their Dickie.

For years the family were drawn for their holidays to the West Country. Often a family party of twenty of them, – uncles, aunts, cousins, nephews and nieces of the McKanes and Godfrees – took three adjacent houses at Rock near Padstow and had a most enjoyable time. The two families were always very close, even though Leslie Godfree had been married before. His first wife had deserted him when he was in France during the first war.

It was in that war that he served in the 331st Brigade of the Royal Horse Artillery. On the day before leaving for France there was a dinner organised for the fifteen officers by the Commanding Officer. Two of them, however, were unable to attend which left thirteen diners for a dinner to be held on a Friday, the 13th. Leslie, the Adjutant, pointed this out to the Commanding Officer: 'I'm not superstitious – are you?' came the answer. 'No sir,' replied Leslie.

The next day the brigade left for France. Four years later the brigade returned home with the same thirteen officers undamaged and Leslie with a Military Cross medal. To celebrate this remarkable survival Leslie ran a reunion dinner party every year for his lucky comrades, a celebration which lasted until 1967 when only three of the original company survived. At that point the annual meeting came to an end. Father Time had taken over.

The years, however, though advancing, have yet to take toll of Kitty. Maybe the fact that she loathes cigarettes is a small something to do with it. A glass of Dubonnet, too, is sufficient to slake her thirst. It was her father who, in her youth, had warned against the vices of drinking and smoking. He had suffered from his own father's over-indulgence which had caused Kitty's father to leave home in his late teens.

Until fairly recently the All-England Club used to give a champagne party on the middle Saturday of the championships. It was then that Kitty's two sons, David and Martin, would force their mother to smoke her one cigarette of the year. It became something of a 'joke for the boys' but it 'quite spoilt the evening for me' she now confesses. 'I felt rather like Liza Doolittle in Shaw's *Pygmalion* when she was being forced to speak "proper".'

Her younger son Martin married into a tennis family. The mother of his wife Helen, was Audrey Cardinall, who was the youngest lady competitor at Wimbledon in the late 1930s, having earlier won the girls' doubles at Junior Wimbledon. Helen, the daughter, has played for the Bank of England, is still the tennis secretary and has been so for the past twelve years. She still plays for both the Bank and for the All-England Club on varying occasions; she is a temporary member of the latter.

Helen wears a Burmese sapphire ring which came to her as an engagement ring from Martin via Kitty's family treasures. A sapphire surrounded by diamonds, it has been in the family for over 150 years and is believed to have come from Kitty's grandparents the Rawsons, the tea planters in Assam.

Martin and Helen, with their young daughter Sophie, live in the same house which Leslie Godfree bought some fifty years ago, just one year before Martin's birth in that house. The house is in East Sheen, by Richmond Park.

Leslie himself died on November 17, 1971, just twenty-four hours after Martin had returned from the United States, especially to see him. He was just on eighty-seven and had enjoyed a very full life. He was a solicitor by profession and a Davis Cup player. He served in two world wars in the Army, on active service in both. His active service in the second world war was happily curtailed by a chance meeting in 1940. Leslie had been in Cherbourg, after Dunkirk, working in a demolition team destroying equipment before the German army arrived. He caught the last boat home a few hours before that event. On arrival back in England, he was posted to Salisbury Plain. He had been there about forty-eight hours when suddenly a voice said: 'Isn't your name Godfree?' It was one of his fellow officers from the first world war. This officer then suggested that Major Godfree was too old to be on active duty in two wars. Leslie was then posted to the War Office for more sedentary duties and transferred to the Intelligence Corps, something which always made him chuckle.

After the war, at the age of sixty-one he joined the sports surface manufacturer En Tout Cas, the company started by an old friend in the 1920s, who had always said if he ever wanted a job, just to let him know. So, in 1946 he did that and Mr Brown took his old friend into his now successful company in which he served actively for twenty-one years. Leslie Godfree, in his active playing years, did much to help Mr Brown in developing the now famous En Tout Cas red tennis court.

In November 1985 the International Lawn Tennis Club of Great Britain and the International Club of France were due to play a match at

Wimbledon on the covered courts. This was a unique occasion because it was the one hundredth match played between the two clubs since they were founded. An even more interesting event occurred at the match for Jean Barotra had played in it without a break from the beginning.

On the Saturday night of the match weekend, there was a dinner to celebrate the occasion. Present at that dinner was Philïpe Chartrier, now President of the French Lawn Tennis Federation. During the after-dinner speeches, Chartrier invited Kitty to go to Paris for the French championships at the Roland Garros stadium and present the ladies' prizes. So from this friendly weekend of tennis and socialising, there came this engaging trip to Paris in the spring.

Christmas 1985 came and was celebrated with the usual full family gathering. New Year's Eve was spent at the All-England Club party dancing the night away.

Unfortunately 1986 did not start too well as Kitty's health slightly deteriorated and she was confined to bed for a few weeks. As always this made her like a caged lioness, wanting to get out and about in the fresh air. However, she rallied and slowly began her recovery. She kept saying 'Oh! Will I make it for my ninetieth birthday, for Paris and for the writing of this book?' She did not want to let anyone down.

She needn't have worried. She celebrated her ninetieth birthday in grand style, a week of parties at varying times. Then there was the prospect of Paris. But the day before her departure she had a prior invitation, issued by the Chairman of the Beckenham Lawn Tennis Club, to open Beckenham's one hundredth anniversary tournament, which, incidentally, Kitty had won sixty-four years previously.

At first she declined the invitation, saying to the Chairman that since she was off to Paris the very next day for a week she really thought it would be too much. But the Chairman was delightfully persuasive finally inviting her to bring a member of her family as escort.

So, once again, not wanting to let anyone down she asked David to escort her. A car arrived from Beckenham and what a day it turned out to be.

On arrival at the ground Kitty was transferred to a Vintage Austin twenty horse-power open tourer on loan from the Syon Park Motor Museum. This car had, in 1930, travelled from London to Cape Town and back, just four years after Kitty had herself been in Cape Town. In this lovely old car Kitty was accompanied by four lady members of the

Beckenham Club, all dressed in 1900-style long dresses and hats and complete with tennis rackets of the era.

The car was driven slowly down the drive and round the ground up to the centre court, whereupon the ladies dressed for tennis alighted and went on court for a demonstration of tennis as played at the turn of the century. Kitty repaired to the VIP's box and the match commenced under the watchful eye of a very colourful umpire, also dressed in the appropriate attire and 'joining in' with the score, with comments and with a sporadic running commentary all done in the light hearted way of sport in a bygone era.

The ladies played well in their very restricting dresses and hats and those 'soggy' rackets. They served underarm of course and as the service was returned, the rallies developed, slowly, and gently with each lady holding the hem of her dress off the ground with her free hand. Those ladies really looked and played the part and Kitty and the crowd thoroughly enjoyed this opening exhibition ceremony. After this Kitty stepped on the court, gave a short address and opened the tournament.

After a very pleasant luncheon and then watching part of the opening match on the centre court, Kitty departed to prepare herself for her week in Paris.

The next morning a car arrived for the journey to London Airport. She was escorted on this trip by Basil Hutchins, a member of the All-England Club committee and the friend who had escorted her to the Olympics in Los Angeles in 1984. So Kitty was off again on another venture.

The flight to Paris was uneventful but the wet and windy weather was most disappointing. Kitty arrived with Basil on June 3, her suitcase full of summer dresses; but luckily she had a warm overcoat which she needed.

Their hotel, La Residence du Bois on the Avenue Grand D'Armée, was a lovely old colonial style building, quiet and most comfortable. There were some friendly faces also staying there from the tennis world, 'Buzzer' Hadingham and his wife, Frank Sedgman and his wife amongst others.

That first night there was a dinner given by the International Tennis Federation for the 1985 world champions Martina Navratilova and Ivan Lendl at the Pavilion Gabriel which was attended by most of the tennis fraternity. This was the first of many engagements.

The next afternoon Kitty and the others walked the ten minutes to the Roland Garros stadium to take their places in the VIP's spectating box. That evening Basil took Kitty to dine in the 'second floor' restaurant of the Eiffel Tower, with its splendid views over Paris and the Seine.

The days passed, full of pleasant events and surprises, until there arrived the men's final. The weather finally had turned warm and it was very pleasant for watching – almost too hot for the sprightly Kitty in the open stadium. But it was a good final which Ivan Lendl won for the second time running. He followed the victory of Chris Lloyd over Navratilova.

The Roland Garros Stadium has recently had a splendid new restaurant built where, as Kitty says, 'we, as guests, were able to select our lunch from a very beautifully laid out large buffet table'.

Then on the Sunday evening came another invitation from Philïpe Chartrier to dinner at La Tour d'Argent at the Quai de la Tournelle. A small gathering this, of the world's tennis greats, where there is a table laid out under a glass dome, just as in June 1867 it was once laid out for Kaiser Wilhelm, his Chancellor Bismarck, Czar Alexander I and his son, later to become Alexander II. They were gathered to see the World Exhibition in Paris. That was a very special evening in an historical setting and Kitty arrived back at her hotel at a quarter to two in the morning.

The taxi arrived at 9 am, the next morning for the trip to the airport for the flight home. Upon arrival in England Kitty went to stay with her son David and his wife Diana so that she could just relax and rest and get cosseted by Diana with breakfast and the *Daily Telegraph* in bed every morning. She needed to get her strength back for the Wimbledon fortnight starting in two weeks time!

Even before Beckenham and Paris another request had been made for Kitty to partake in yet another tournament, this time from her grandson, Jonathan. He is a civil engineer who works for DOW Chemicals and his company sponsored the Birmingham Edgbaston tournament. Jonathan asked her in January of 1986 if she would consider going to Birmingham to present the prizes to which request she readily agreed.

The arrangements were made and Jonathan was to drive his Grandmother to Birmingham on the Sunday morning, to arrive in time for lunch, watch the finals, present the prizes and then drive back home –

a long day for a ninety year old. But she was game.

Then came a change in plan. DOW, appreciating the situation, cut the travelling drastically. Instead of collecting his grandmother and driving to Birmingham, Jonathan drove her to Redhill airport where both of them stepped aboard a helicopter for the ride to Birmingham. The helicopter then put down on the tennis court!

The greetings over, luncheon was taken and the ladies' final was played. The event was won by Pam Shriver. Kitty presented the trophies and, having done her bit, the helicopter re-appeared for the return journey.

But this time the Vice President of DOW Europe and his wife were on board because they were to be taken to London Airport and dropped off, to catch a scheduled flight to Zurich. This small diversion proved to be a rather exciting adventure because a helicopter coming from the provinces is not exactly the most popular of aircraft with the flight controllers at London airport. However, the diversion and drop off were made without incident.

On the way from London Airport back to Redhill the pilot of the helicopter confirmed that the whole exercise had been an unusual experience for him too, because, as he said, he had never flown a 'chopper' into London airport before. Kitty is still achieving 'firsts' and still enjoying it all.

Invitations to weddings, celebration lunches and dinners still drop through her letter box. Wimbledon mounted a special lunch in May 1986, with Kitty as guest of honour on her ninetieth birthday, and sixty years since her second winning of the title in 1926. All this worried her in advance, still a shy schoolgirl at heart.

Earlier in April of the same year, the All-England Club held their annual dinner for male members only. But when Virginia Wade was elected to the Committee two or three years ago, she was entitled to join the dinner where she found herself the lone female among some 200 men. Last Spring, however, Kitty was invited to join the dinner which relieved Virginia of her somewhat lonely position.

Although the invitations underline both the affection and respect in which the public hold Kitty, one must not forget that there is, and always has been, a private, family life too. Kitty has never stinted in giving love and devotion to those close to her.

In September 1965 her elder son had a very bad car accident from which, at first, there was serious doubt about his chances of recovery.

However, all was well in the end, although he is not the most active member of the family.

Unfortunately David's wife at the time, found it impossible to carry on. So at the age of seventy, Kitty and husband Leslie, then eighty-one, opened their doors to David again, but this time with his two young children, Jonathan and Sarah, then aged about six and five respectively.

'Grandma' then set about bringing up two youngsters once again, this time her grandchildren.

A local school was selected for them and after the two fairly shattering experiences, Kitty set out to rebuild those young lives. She worked ceaselessly at everything children demand as a routine. But in addition every afternoon, when they came home from school, she sat down with each one in turn and carried out a form of debriefing of the schoolday's events and anything they did not understand she explained. She taught them the 'three R's' so quickly that they forged ahead at school by the second term.

She taught them how to swim with regular visits to Richmond Baths. She taught them the rudiments of cricket and of tennis, but above all, she gave them a stable existence and let them regain their confidence.

This went on for some three years, until 1969 when David remarried. His bride was his schooldays sweetheart Diana. She gradually took on the onerous task of following Kitty. Between them they did a magnificent job, with Kitty acting as the 'Rock of Gibraltar' which she has always been.

In addition to all this, she was also running the home which included husband Leslie, second son Martin and two dogs. But she happily took the whole thing in her stride.

Indeed, to take things in her stride has always been second nature to Kitty – on the tennis court, in public, and in the privacy of her family life. In her ninety-first year there came all those tiring public functions, the presentation ceremonies at Birmingham, Beckenham and Paris and most treasured of all, the ceremony on the centre court of her beloved Wimbledon with the Duke and Duchess of Kent. Some retirement!

Every day appears to be a springboard to Kitty's future. She seems to explore the astonishment of living as she absorbs the poetry of the everyday. She is, I suggest, the quintessence of dust and with her devoted proud family I trust she continues to imprison that little shadow in the grass for some time to come.

Bibliography

Crowded Galleries by Dame Norma Brookes, William Heinemann Ltd.,
   1956.

Kathleen Godfree by Alan Little, The Wimbledon Lawn Tennis Museum,
   1984.

The Changing Face of Wimbledon by Alan Little, The Wimbledon Lawn
Tennis Museum, 1986

Record of Major Competition Results

THE CHAMPIONSHIPS WIMBLEDON

(The dates represent the starting day of the championships – the numbers of letters in brackets represent the round number of the tournament. In doubles and mixed doubles the partner's name is shown.)

Worple Road

1919 – JUNE 23

Singles	(1)	Bt Miss O B Manser	6–3, 7–5
	(2)	Bt Mrs F C Colston	6–2, 6–2
	(3)	Bt Mrs King	6–1, 6–2
	(QF)	Lost to Mlle S Lenglen	0–6, 1–6

Doubles (QF) Mrs C R Satterthwaite

Mixed (3) C Tindall Green

1920 – JUNE 21

Singles	(1)	A bye	
	(2)	Bt Miss E L Colyer	6–2, 4–6, 6–3
	(3)	Lost to Mrs R J McNair	3–6, 6–4, 2–6

Doubles (QF) Mrs R J McNair

Mixed (QF) G R Sherwell

1921 – JUNE 20

Singles (1) Bt Mrs H Edgington   6–2, 6–4
         (2) Lost to Miss E Ryan   4–6, 2–6

Mixed   (1) L A Godfree

W i m b l e d o n

1922 – JUNE 26

Singles (1) Bt Miss E Sears   6–1, 6–1
         (2) Lost to Mlle S Lenglen   1–6, 5–7

Doubles (F) Mrs A D Stocks

Mixed   (QF) W C Crawley

1923 – JUNE 25

Singles (1) Bt Miss K L Gardner   6–1, 6–0
         (2) Bt Miss P Holcroft   6–1, 6–2
         (3) Bt Miss A Rodacanachi   6–0, 6–1
         (4) Bt Mrs R C Clayton   6–4, 6–1
         (QF) Bt Miss E Goss   6–2, 6–2
         (SF) Bt Miss E Ryan   1–6, 6–2, 6–4
         (F) Lost to Mlle S Lenglen   2–6, 2–6

Doubles (SF) Mrs L Chambers

Mixed   (QF) W C Crawley

1924 – JUNE 21

Singles (1) Bt Mrs F C Colston   6–4, 4–6, 6–1
         (2) Bt Mrs M Mallory   6–1, 6–0
         (3) Bt Miss D H Woolrych   4–6, 6–0, 6–0
         (QF) Bt Mrs J B Jessop   6–1, 6–3
         (SF) Bt Mlle Lenglen   W O
         (F) Bt Miss H Wills   4–6, 6–4, 6–4

Doubles (Final) Mrs B C Covell
Mixed   (Winner) J B Gilbert

1 9 2 5 – J U N E 2 2

Singles (1) Bt Miss G R Starry   6–3, 6–1
        (2) Bt Mrs A V Bridge   6–0, 6–1
        (3) Bt Mrs Satterthwaite   6–1, 6–1
        (QF) Bt Miss E Boyd   6–1, 6–1
        (SF) Lost to Mlle S Lenglen   0–6, 0–6

Doubles (2) Miss P Saunders

Mixed (QF) J B Gilbert

1 9 2 6 – J U N E 2 1

Singles (1) Bt Mrs Van Ellison   6–0, 6–0
        (2) Bt Miss D H Woolrych   6–2, 6–0
        (3) Bt Miss E Ryan   1–6, 6–4, 6–0
        (QF) Bt Miss C Tyrell   6–2, 6–0
        (SF) Bt Mlle Vlasto   6–4, 6–0
        (F) Bt Snra L de Alvarez   6–2, 4–6, 6–3

Doubles (F) Miss E L Colyer

Mixed (Winner) L A Godfree bt Kinsey and
                Miss M K Browne   6–3, 6–4

1 9 2 7 – J U N E 2 0

Singles (1) A Bye
        (2) Bt Miss N Trentham   6–2, 6–2
        (3) Bt Miss R D Tapscott   6–2, 10–8
        (4) Bt Miss E L Colyer   6–2, 6–2
        (QF) Lost to Miss E Ryan   6–3, 4–6, 4–6

Doubles (SF) Miss B Nuthall

Mixed (F) L A Godfree

1 9 2 8 – J U N E 2 2

No Wimbledon entry.
Recovering from appendix operation.

1929 – JUNE 20

No Wimbledon entry.
Arrival of first born.

1930 – JUNE 23

Mixed (2)   L A Godfree

1931 – JUNE 22

Singles (1)   Bt Miss J Jedrzeiowska   2–6, 6–4, 6–3
         (2)   Bt Miss I Adamoff   6–3, 6–4
         (3)   Bt Mrs J S Kirk   6–2, 6–0
         (4)   Lost to Miss H Jacobs   2–6, 1–6

Doubles (SF)   Miss D Round

Mixed (2)   J S Olliff

1932 – JUNE 21

Singles(1)   1A Bye
         (2)   Bt Miss R E Haylock   6–2, 6–8, 6–3
         (3)   Bt Mrs H A Lewis   6–4, 6–2
         (4)   Lost to Miss F S Moody   3–6, 0–6

Doubles (2)   Miss G R Sterry

Mixed (2)   C H Kingsley

1933 – JUNE 26

Singles (1)   Bt Miss S Rosambert   5–7, 6–2, 6–4
         (2)   Lost to Miss M C Scriven   2–6, 6–1, 3–6

Doubles (SF)   Mrs L R C Mitchell

Mixed (SF)   C H Kingsley

1934 – JUNE 25

Singles (1) Bt Miss J Saunders   6–3, 8–6
        (2) Bt Miss F S Ford   6–1, 6–0
        (3) Lost to Miss S Palfrey   3–6, 1–6

Doubles (SF)   Miss M C Scriven

Mixed (QF)   C H Kingsley

THE WIGHTMAN CUP

1923 – FOREST HILLS, NEW YORK – AUGUST 11 AND 13

Singles   Lost to Miss H Wills   2–6, 5–7
         Lost to Mrs F Mallory   2–6, 3–6

Doubles   (Mrs B C Covell) lost to
         Mrs G Wightman and Miss E Goss
            8–10, 7–5, 4–6

US Won 7—0

1924 – WIMBLEDON – JUNE 18 AND 19

Singles   Bt Mrs F Mallory   6–3, 6–3
         Bt Miss H Wills   6–2, 6–2

Doubles   (Miss E L Colyer) lost to
         Mrs G Wightman, and Miss H Wills
            6–2, 2–6, 4–6

GB Won 6—1

1925 – FOREST HILLS, NEW YORK – AUGUST 14 AND 15

Singles   Bt Mrs F Mallory   6–4, 5–7, 6–0
         Lost to Miss H Wills   1–6, 6–1, 7–9

Doubles   (Miss E L Colyer) bt Miss H Wills and
         Miss M K Browne   6–0, 6–3

GB Won 4—3

1 9 2 6 – WIMBLEDON – JUNE 1 7 AND 1 8

Singles Bt Miss M K Browne   6–1, 7–5
           Bt Miss E Ryan   6–1, 5–7, 6–4

Doubles (Miss E L Colyer) lost to
           Miss M K Browne and
           Miss E Ryan   6–3, 2–6, 4–6

US Won 4—3

1 9 2 7 – FOREST HILLS – AUGUST 1 2 AND 1 3

Singles Lost to Mrs F Mallory   4–6, 2–6
           Lost to Miss H Wills   1–6, 1–6

Doubles (Miss E H Harvey) lost to
           Miss H Wills and
           Mrs H Wightman   4–6, 6–4, 3–6

US Won 5—2

1 9 3 0 – WIMBLEDON – JUNE 1 3 AND 1 4

Doubles (Mrs P Holcroft Watson)
           bt Mrs H Moody and
           Miss H Jacobs   7–5, 1–6, 6–4

GB Won 4—3

1 9 3 4 – WIMBLEDON – JUNE 1 5 AND 1 6

Doubles (Miss B Nuthall) lost to
           Miss H Jacobs and
           Miss S Palfrey   7–5, 3–6, 2–6

US Won 5—2

THE OLYMPIC GAMES

1920 — ANTWERP, HOLLAND — AUGUST 15

Singles (1) Bt Mrs Vaussard   6–4, 6–4
         (2) Bt Mlle Gagliardi   6–1, 1–6, 6–0
         (QF) Bt Mlle D'Ayen   6–2, 6–0
         (SF) Lost to Miss E D Holman W O
         (Third place play off) Bt Mme Fick   6–2, 6–0

Doubles (Winner) Mrs R J McNair

Mixed (F) M Woosam

1924 — PARIS — JULY 13

Singles (1) A Bye
         (2) Bt Mme de Borman   6–0, 6–2
         (3) Bt Mme Fick   6–1, 6–1
         (QF) Bt Mrs J B Jessop   6–2, 6–0
         (SF) Lost to Mlle D Vlasto   6–0, 5–7, 1–6
         (Third place play off) Bt Mme Golding   5–7, 6–3, 6–0

Doubles (F) Mrs B C Covell

Mixed (SF) J B Gilbert (Withdrew from third place play off).

UNITED STATES CHAMPIONSHIPS

1923 — FOREST HILLS, NEW YORK — AUGUST 13–18

Singles (1) Bt Miss L Dixon   6–1, 6–2
         (2) Bt Mrs LeRoy   6–1, 6–0
         (3) Bt Mrs Shedden   6–1, 6–1
         (QF) Lost to Miss H Wills   6–2, 2–6, 5–7

Doubles (Winner) Mrs B C Covell
         Bt Mrs G Wightman and Miss E Goss   2–6, 6–3, 6–1

1923 — LONGWOOD CC, BOSTON — AUGUST 20

Mixed Doubles (F) J B Hawkes

1 9 2 5 – FOREST HILLS, NEW YORK – AUGUST 1 7

Singles (1) Bt Mrs J S Taylor 6–2, 6–0
         (2) Bt Mrs Godfrey   6–1, 6–0
         (3) Bt Miss J B Jessop   6–0, 6–0
         (QF) Bt Miss E Ryan   3–6, 7–5, 6–2
         (SF) Bt Mrs F Mallory   4–6, 7–5, 8–6
         (F) Lost to Miss H Wills   6–3, 0–6, 2–6

Doubles (QF) Miss E L Colyer

1 9 2 5 – LONGWOOD CC, BOSTON – AUGUST 2 4

Mixed Doubles (Winner) J B Hawkes
            Bt V Richards and Miss E H Harvey   6–2, 6–4

1 9 2 7 – FOREST HILLS, NEW YORK – AUGUST 2 2

Doubles (Winner) Miss E H Harvey
        Bt Miss J Fry and Miss B Nuthall   6–1, 4–6, 6–4.

FRENCH CHAMPIONSHIPS

1 9 2 5 – ST CLOUD, PARIS – MAY 2 7

Singles (1) A Bye
         (2) Bt Miss Rosenbaum   6–2, 6–1
         (3) Bt Mlle Deve   6–1, 6–2
         (QF) Bt Mme Billout   6–0, 10–8
         (SF) Bt Mlle D Vlasto   6–2, 6–2
         (F) Lost to Mlle S Lenglen   1–6, 2–6

Doubles (F) Miss E L Colyer

Mixed (2) C G Eames

1 9 2 6 – PARIS – JUNE 2

Singles (1) Bt Mlle de Borman   6–1, 6–2
         (2) Bt Mlle G Grassett   6–4, 6–4
         (QF) Lost to Miss M K Browne   5–7, 0–6

Doubles (F) Miss E L Colyer

Mixed (SF) L A Godfree

WORLD'S HARD COURT CHAMPIONSHIPS

1922 – BRUSSELS – MAY 13

Singles (1) A Bye
(2) Bt Mlle Gagliardi   6–0, 6–1
(3) Bt Mme Grisar   6–0, 6–1
(QF) Bt Mrs C R Satterthwaite   7–5, 6–2
(SF) Lost to Mlle S Lenglen   8–10, 2–6

Doubles (F) Mrs A E Beamish

Mixed (SF) H R Barrett

1923 – ST CLOUD, PARIS – MAY 19

Singles (1) Bt Mlle Y Bourgeois   6–2, 6–1
(2) Bt Mlle B Amblard   6–0, 6–0
(3) Bt Mme Storms   6–1, 6–1
(QF) Bt Mme Billout   6–2, 7–5
(SF) Bt Mme Golding   6–2, 6–2
(F) Lost to Mlle S Lenglen   3–6, 3–6

Doubles (Winner) Mrs A E Beamish

Mixed (F) J B Gilbert

WORLD'S COVERED COURT CHAMPIONSHIPS

1919 – PARIS – NOVEMBER 15

Singles (1) Bt Miss P Hawkins   6–0, 6–4
(2) Bt Miss Vanssard   6–3, 6–2
(SF) Lost to Miss E D Holman   2–6, 4–6

Doubles (Winner) Mrs A E Beamish

Mixed (SF) H Portlock

1920 — QUEENS CLUB — OCTOBER 11

Singles (1) Bt Mme Prince Miville   6–0, 6–0
           (2) Bt Mrs I Knight   6–1, 6–0
           (QF) Bt Mrs E B Warburg   6–3, 6–1
           (SF) Bt Miss E D Holman   1–6, 6–1, 6–3
           (F) Lost to Mrs A E Beamish   3–6, 7–5, 7–9

Doubles (Winner) Mrs A E Beamish

Mixed (F) S N Doust

1923 — BARCELONA — FEBRUARY 1

Singles (1) A Bye
           (2) Bt Mme Billout WO
           (QF) Bt Srta Torras   6–0, 6–1
           (SF) Bt Mme Vaussard   6–2, 6–2
           (F) Bt Mrs A E Beamish   6–3, 4–6, 6–2

Doubles (Winner) Mrs A E Beamish

Mixed (Winner) W C Crawley

HARD COURT CHAMPIONSHIPS OF GREAT BRITAIN

1934 — BOURNEMOUTH — APRIL 30

Doubles (Winner) Miss S Noel

Mixed (1) C H Kingsley